ADVERTISING YOUR BUSINESS MADE E-Z

Garrett Adams

MADE E-Z PRODUCTS, Inc.
Deerfield Beach, Florida / www.MadeE-Z.com

Advertising Your Business Made E-Z™
© 2000 Made E-Z Products, Inc.
Printed in the United States of America

MADE E-Z
PRODUCTS

384 South Military Trail
Deerfield Beach, FL 33442
Tel. 954-480-8933
Fax 954-480-8906
http://www.MadeE-Z.com

1 2 3 4 5 6 7 8 9 10   CPC   R   10 9 8 7 6 5 4 3 2

Advertising Your Business Made E-Z™
By Garrett Adams

Table of contents

Introduction to Advertising Your Business Made E-Z™

A strange thing happens when you don't advertise—*nothing.*

This book shows you how to conquer the complex and often baffling world of advertising and public relations. Build your business by using powerful promotion and public relations strategies to gain maximum exposure for your product or service. Learn how to successfully combine the right words with the right media—print, TV, radio, classified, mail order, even infomercials—for dynamic low-cost advertising strategies that get results.

The past decade has seen explosive growth in a dynamic new marketing direction—infomercials. Learn how to produce your own infomercial from concept and casting to shooting and distribution. Analyze your market and select the TV station that best fits your needs and budget. Use celebrities, testimonials, and joint ventures—all the secrets of the "profs"—to increase your profits and effectively and affordably reach your customers.

A veritable encyclopedia of proven advertising and promotion strategies for any type business, and any size budget—Made E-Z!

Basics of promotion and advertising

1

Chapter 1

Basics of promotion and advertising

Promotion advertising differs significantly from consumer franchise-building advertising. The franchise-building ads are long-term in nature and aimed at giving customers reasons to buy.

note Promotion advertising is short-term. It pushes for the order by providing incentives, coupons, rebates, premiums and contests.

As a rule, promotion advertising should be short-term, specific and call only for consumers to perform a desired action. Resist including extraneous points in the promotional ad. Focus on a simple "call to action."

The most common medium for promotion advertising is print. Some big-budget advertisers use broadcast (radio and television) to persuade consumers to look for their promotion advertising in their local newspapers.

For example: Your ad copy may ask the readers to:

- redeem a coupon and save $2

- buy two packs and get the third one free

- fill out a coupon and enter sweepstakes to win $100,000

- buy two products and receive a free gift worth $10

Most promotion events are price or added-value oriented campaigns. As such, it is important that when writing copy, the ad should appeal more to the wallet than the emotion.

CAUTION Do not make your redemption procedure complicated and confusing.

Also, avoid a more than one-time offers in which the consumer is forced to use math in order to determine which ones save more money. Your task is to make it easy for the consumer. Avoid having to make them decide. That's too much work for them.

16 ideas for low-cost promotion

Promotion and advertising can be a heavy expense, especially for a new business that wants to make itself known in a community. A home-based business however, more often than not, has a very limited budget when it comes to advertising. The home business owner needs to make the public aware of his or her product or service at the lowest possible cost.

There are many ways. A pet breeder in a large city was struggling for several years, until he came up with a novel idea. He started giving away customized "birth certificates" for the pets he sold. Almost immediately, his sales rose more than 10 percent.

The owner of a new home cleaning service was trying to attract clients. She couldn't afford much advertising, so she began offering "home cleaning seminars" to civic groups. After two months of seminars, she was swamped with inquiries and clients.

Customers or clients must know about a business or product line before they'll buy and they must have a reason to buy. If you are trying to promote your business now, you can move in one of two directions:

1) You can take the conventional route to promotion and mount an elaborate media campaign, spending a considerable amount of money.

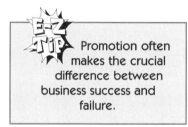

Promotion often makes the crucial difference between business success and failure.

2) You can let your creative juices flow and mount a low-cost promotion effort, using a potpourri of attention-getting gimmicks to bring your message to the buying public.

Now, to be sure, conventional advertising is valuable. If your enterprise is large enough or if you're selling numerous product lines, you may find that a full-fledged media campaign is the most efficient and cost effective way to promote your business.

If money is tight, however, or you're not sure you can pay for the heavy cost of a media campaign over a period of time, there are an assortment of low-cost techniques you can try. Not all may be appropriate for your particular business, and certainly it would be costly to try them all. But you're sure to find some ideas that will work for you. Use sixteen these low-cost promotion techniques:

1) Giveaways

People love to receive "free" items, especially items they can use to gain knowledge or improve their lives. You can base an entire promotional campaign on this desire. If you're running a furniture repair business, for instance, you could give away a furniture repair brochure, free furniture planning guides, or color swatches. Once you begin giving away authoritative information, customers will begin to perceive you as an expert in your field.

2) News creation

Do you want to get names and news from your business in the local newspaper? It may be easier than you think. If you don't have any news to report to the local media, create some. Maybe you've taken on a new associate. Or maybe you're selling an unusual product line. Or maybe you've opened a free advice center for the community. Or maybe you've received an award from a civic or professional group.

Local weeklies and pennysavers are often quite interested in business news and can help you attract the attention of thousands of people.

3) Events

You may be able to attract the attention of a crowd or the media by staging a special promotional event. If you run fitness classes, for instance, you could stage a celebrity instructor day. If you're promoting a new real estate business, you can offer tours of a model home in the area. If you're selling children's products and it's springtime, you can offer lunch with the Easter bunny. Get the idea?

4) Charity tie-ins

Are you launching a new product? Trying to increase visibility among a particular segment of your community? Offer your product to one or more local charities as a raffle prize or for use at a fund-raising event. You'll receive lots of exposure among people who buy tickets or attend the event.

5) Contests

Offer a desirable or unique item—or even several items—as contest prizes. First, find a contest theme that ties into your business. A caterer might offer a quiche-eating contest. A photographer might offer a young model contest. A mail order craft firm might offer an "Early American" handicrafts contest. Invite contest submissions and offer prizes to the winners. Do contests attract attention? You bet. All it takes is a few signs, a small press announcement or two, and the word will spread throughout the community grapevine.

6) Community service

Ask yourself how your enterprise can be a "good neighbor" to your community. If you're running a lawn care and gardening service, perhaps you can offer one season's services at no charge to a needy charitable organization or nursing home in your area. Hundreds of people will hear about your work in the process. Volunteer for various community causes. If appropriate, you can step in during community emergency, offering products and services to help an organization or individuals in need.

note Nothing brings you to the attention of the people faster, or more favorably, than community service.

7) Couponing

Americans are very coupon-conscious. Test the market. At what level will coupons increase the volume of various product or service lines? When you get some tentative answers, start distributing coupons that offer a discount on your services. Distribute them to area newspapers, on store counters, in door-to-door mail packets (which can often be quite inexpensive), at the public library, at laundromats—at any location where people congregate.

8) Badges and novelties

You can easily and inexpensively produce badges, bumper stickers, book covers, and other novelty items for distribution in your area. You can imprint your business name and the first names of the customers on many of these products at little cost and distribute them for free. You can tie your novelty program into a contest: once a month, you can offer a prize to any individual whose car happens to carry one of your bumper stickers or badges with peel-off coupons, redeemable at your place of business.

9) Celebrity visits

With a bit of persistence, you may be able to arrange to have a local media celebrity, public official, entertainment personality, or even a fictitious cartoon character or clown visit your business. The celebrity can sign autographs, read stories to children, perform cooking demonstrations, or perform any one of a hundred other traffic-building activities.

10) Celebrate holidays

You'll probably want to celebrate major public holidays with special sales. Almost every business has a few little-known holidays. Ever hear of National Pickle Day, for instance? Or Cat Lovers Month? Once you find the "right" holiday, you can sponsor a special sale or special product, and arrange media coverage of a holiday event.

11) Go where the people are

You can open sales information booths at community fairs and festivals. This promotional technique can work for gift retailers, craftspeople, and personal service firms. If you have the people and the time, can you handle regional fairs or even trade shows?

12) Mailing lists

Once you begin establishing a committed clientele, gather their names on a mailing list. Save the names from your mail orders and telephone inquiries. Eventually, you'll be able to send product circulars or even catalogs to the folks on your list and you'll be able to promise your products by mail.

13) Unbeatable deals

If you want people to buy NOW, offer them an unbeatable deal. If they bring an old product—a small appliance, a book, or whatever to you—give them a worthwhile discount on a comparable new item. Or, stage a general purpose scavenger hunt with a surprise party at the end or special gift incentive and offer discounts to the winners. Another idea: customers who bring in three canned goods for your community's food bank receive a discount on products purchased that day.

14) Parties

Everyone loves a party. If you're running a service business, perhaps you can offer an open house or obtain a small banquet room in your community. Besides offering refreshments, be sure the place is brightly decorated.

15) Greeting cards

Do you send greeting cards to major customers or clients? Holidays, birthdays, and anniversaries make nice greeting card occasions. Greeting cards create enormous goodwill and keep your name in front of people.

Why not celebrate the anniversary of your business or some special holiday by offering baked goods and beverages?

16) Seminars

In this information-hungry age, people love to receive advice, especially about their personal needs and hobbies. If you sell health foods or run fitness classes, perhaps you can offer "wellness" seminars during lunchtime to your area's business community. If you're an interior decorator, perhaps you can offer one-hour decorating workshops to any group of ten people who will gather in someone's home. If you're running a printing business, perhaps you can offer tours and layout seminars at your plant.

If you're not pleased with your promotional efforts today or if you simply must increase your exposure among customers and prospects—it's probably time to increase your publicity efforts.

By all means, advertise in the media if you can. Ponder the products, services, and events you can offer the community and devise a creative promotional strategy around them. You'll have to invest a bit of time and energy in the project, but the payoff will be worth it. You'll save hundreds— or even thousands—of advertising dollars and, better yet, you'll travel a well-worn shortcut to profit.

The inside secrets of free publicity for your business

Product publicity is the "secret pathway" to the business success everyone wants. In simple terms, product publicity is a kind of advertising that costs you nothing, yet brings in the orders for you.

Regardless of what kind of business you are operating, you should strive for as much publicity for your business and your products or services as possible. After all, it's "free advertising" that is essential to the

Don't neglect your greatest promotional asset— your mind.

growth of your business. However, your publicity efforts should be well thought out, and pre-planned for maximum results.

DEFINITION

The first, and most basic form for obtaining publicity, is through what is known as the *press* or *news release*. This is generally a one page story about your business, your product/service or an event/happening related to your business that has or is about to occur. These publicity stories are generally "shot-gunned" to all the various media: local newspapers, radio and TV, and trade publications.

Problem number one is getting the people to whom you sent these publicity stories to use, publish, or broadcast them. And, this leads us to the right way of writing publicity stories:

In every case, send a short cover letter addressed to the person who you want to consider your material. This means that you send your story to the city editor of the newspapers; the news directors of the radio and TV stations, and the managing editors of the various trade publications. It will do you no good what so ever, to send your material to the advertising, circulation or business managers if you describe how you're a long-time advertiser, subscriber or listener. The most important thing is that you make contact with the person

who has the final say as to what is to be published or broadcast and, at the bottom line, that this person's use of your material will somehow make him a "hero" to the readers, viewers or listeners.

The cover letter should be a short note. Go to a paper supplier—

"From the desk of . . ." note sheets are too elaborate until the people you're contacting get to know you.

tell him you want a hundred or so sheets of good bond paper—8-1/2 by 11" preferably in a pastel color such as blue or ivory. You want this paper cut into quarters, giving you a grand total of 400 sheets of note paper.

On this note sheet, begin with the date across the top, skip a couple of spaces, and then quickly tell the recipient of the note that the attached material is new and should be of real interest to his readers, viewers or listeners.

Dealers and distributors should send the following note to the editors and news directors of the media in their area: "Here's something that's new, and truly helpful for a change, to people trying to cope with inflation and soaring living costs—as well as those engaged in building extra income businesses of their own. This should be of real value and interest to your readers. Please take a look. If you have any questions, or if you need more information, please call me at: (123) 456-7890." Then, of course, you skip about four spaces, type your name, your business name, and your address. Sign your name above where you typed it, and staple this note in the upper right hand corner of your news release. This note must be typed and double-spaced.

So, now you've got a cover letter, and you know to whom to send it. Type one note, and take it to a nearby quick-print shop. They copy the note 4 times, paste these 4 copies onto one sheet of paper, print 50 to 100 copies, and cut the paper into individual notes, all inexpensively priced.

Now you need the actual publicity release, which must be "properly" written if you expect it to be used by the media. Above all else, there's a proper form or style to use—plus the fact that it must be typed, double-spaced, and short—about a half page in total length.

note You attract attention and interest with the headline and fill in the details with your story.

From the left margin, about an inch from the top of the paper, with an inch and a half margin on each side of the paper; type in all capital letters: PRESS RELEASE: Underline these words. Immediately following the colon, but not in all capital letters, put in the date. Always set the date forward by at least one day after the day you intend to mail the release.

On the same line, but on the right hand side of the page, and in all capital letters, write the words, FOR FURTHER INFORMATION: Underline this, and immediately below, but not in all capital letters, type your name, your phone number, and your address.

Skip a couple of spaces, then in all capital letters—centered between the margins—type a story headline, and underline it. Skip a couple of spaces, and from the left hand margin, all in capital letters, type the words, FOR IMMEDIATE RELEASE: From there on, it's the news or publicity story itself.

You can write the headline before the story, and then a story to fit the headline—or, write the story before the headline, and then write a headline to fit the story—either way, it's basically the same as writing a space ad or a sales letter.

Here's an example of the headline used for a publicity blurb:

HELP MAKE ENDS MEET—NEW PUBLICATION FOR
EXTRA INCOME SEEKERS

Notice how it continues to sell or involve the editor. Readers are always looking for better ways to make ends meet, and they're specifically interested in what your promise involves. The editor wants readers to "think well" of him for enlightening them with this source of help, so he reads the story to find out who, what and how.

Your headline, and the story you present, must sell the editor on the benefits of your product or service to his readers. Unless it specifically does this, an editor won't use it. The person you send your press or publicity release to must quickly see and understand how your product or service will benefit readers, thereby making him a "hero" to them—an editor must be assured it will do what you promise in your headline.

You must sell the first person receiving your materials. Keep this fact uppermost in your mind as you write it.

Come right to the point and say your product is lower in price, more convenient to use, or how your product or service is useful. It's also a good idea to include a complimentary sample of your product or an opportunity for a reviewer, writer, or editor to sample your services.

Remember, the editors receiving your information are fully aware of your purposes—free advertising! They are not interested in you or your credentials. If you sold them on the benefits of your business, service, or product to their

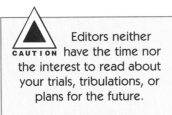

Editors neither have the time nor the interest to read about your trials, tribulations, or plans for the future.

readers, and they want background details, they'll call you. That's why you list your telephone number and address.

Editors are busy—they only want "a flag" that alerts them to something new and of probable interest to their readers. Sell the editor first. Convince him that you found the better mousetrap. Show an editor that your product or service fills a need and will interest a large segment of readers, viewers, or listeners.

Never send a publicity release to an editor and then call or write complaining—demanding to know why he either didn't use it or why he changed it. Do this once, and that particular media will "round-file" any further material received from you—unopened! If your first effort is not used, then review the story yourself. Perhaps write it from a different angle, make sure you're sending it to the proper person—and try again!

Editors handle hundreds of publicity releases passing across their desks every day. They only have so much space or time. Therefore, your material has to stand out and in some way fit with the information the editors want to pass along to their readers, viewers, or listeners. Regardless of your business, product, or service, you must build your press release around that particular angle or feature that makes it beneficial or of interest to the media you want to run your press release. Without this special ingredient, you're lost before you begin.

A story about job lay-offs and increased unemployment would prompt a publicity release to all the media on the help and opportunity offered by, for example, MONEY MAKING MAGIC! Say there's a deluge of chain letters and pyramid schemes making the rounds—the media picks up on it and attempts to warn the people to beware. Within 5 days, issue a publicity release, explaining the availability of this report on chain letters and pyramid schemes—a report that explains everything from A to Z—who are the winners and losers.

There's also another kind of timing to keep in mind—publication deadlines. For best results, always try to time it so your material reaches the editor in time for the Sunday paper. That's when the papers have their greatest circulation, the most space is available, and people have the most time to read the paper.

When an editor uses your publicity release, always follow-up with a short thank you note.

For articles you'd like to appear in the Sunday paper, you'll generally have to get your release in at least nine days prior to the date of publication. If you're in doubt, call and ask about the deadline date.

In summary

✦ Choose the media most likely to carry your press release. Select those that regularly carry similar write-ups.

✦ Always use a cover letter of some kind. It pays to call ahead to find out the correct name of the person to whom you should direct your press release.

✦ Use the proper press release form, complete with a headline that will interest the decision-maker.

✦ Be sure your press release is letter perfect—no typos or misspelled words—and don't photo-copy. Always have each letter or press release individually typed or printed.

✦ When your item is used, send a thank you note or call the editor on the phone and thank him for using your press release.

✦ Never, but never, call or write editors demanding to know why they didn't use your press release, why they had it rewritten or cut it short—just try, and try again!

Writing successful ads

Chapter 2

Writing successful ads

The words "press release" seem to scare most people. In fact, not many people take the time to even think of writing their own press release.

A press release needs to "inform" people, NOT sell them something. For example, you are reading this because you want to learn something that will *benefit you.* You aren't reading this just so you can buy something else. If money is the driving force in your business—you won't go too far. Your main goals should be pleasing customers, providing them with a high-quality product, more than their money's worth. The trick is to do all this while still making money. People don't care what mountains you had to climb, or what seas you had to cross.

> **note** The first thing you have to remember is that a press release is a "news" item.

note

The sales circulars you print and mail will sell your product. A *press release* informs others about your product. Instead of your main objective being to sell the product and have the customer send in an order immediately, a press release informs the customer exactly how your product will benefit their lives. This must be conveyed in the form of a "newsworthy" press release. If you have a sales circular to sell a product, you can easily turn it into a press release without much difficulty. It's just a new marketing angle of presenting your product to the public.

The following is an example of a typical press release:

FOR IMMEDIATE RELEASE   CONTACT NAME
ISSUE DATE   ADDRESS
                                                       PHONE

PRESS RELEASE HEADLINE

Many people are entering the mail order market these days, but getting ripped-off by a bunch of hype. People are promised untold riches in a short period of time. The hype ads play with their emotions by making them believe it's easy to make money through the mail. It's sad.

However, a new book was just been released to help solve these problems—for the first time in history—a REAL directory was compiled, listing the name and addresses of 179 honest and trustworthy mail order folks. People can write and receive FREE information to get them started in their own business now!

You can get this book for only $4.95. Meet the real mail order dealers who care about their products and want to help you get started doing what they are doing.

For more information and to order the book (*provide contact information*).

- END -

This was a short press release—however, you should be able to see the "newsworthiness" in it. Its main focus is on the fact that most people get ripped-off when they start their first mail order business. The solution to this problem is a new directory that is available for the first time in history. The sell builds slowly because the reader will naturally want to get his hands on this one. It doesn't ask for money, it only tells the reader how to get a copy if he wants one.

Here's a great test for a press release: Since your final sales pitch is included in the last paragraph—read the press release aloud. Would it still be worth reading without your sales pitch? If so, it's probably a press release.

Press releases come in many forms depending upon the product you are writing about. However, the basic rule of thumb still applies. If you never wrote one before—it may be a little difficult. Don't despair. Grab the latest daily newspaper and read some of their informational articles. Notice how each article is written and pattern yours after the same format. After you do a few of them, you'll be able to "get the picture."

When your press release is written to your satisfaction, the proper way to submit it to a publisher is:

- Type it on a typewriter or computer. Standard format is double-spaced and not longer than two 8-1/2 x 11 pages.

- Put your name, address and page number at the top of each page.

- Write the note: "For Immediate Release" at the top. If you are only sending the press release to one publication—tell them it's a "first run."

How to avoid common advertising mistakes

Advertising isn't hard to do. You prepare an advertisement or write a classified ad to sell your product or generate interest to send people more information. Here are some pointers to follow:

Writing effective copy

Never try to sell anything costing more than $5 in a small display or classified ad. First of all, you don't have enough room to tell people everything they need to know to entice them to order.

Instead, you need to employ the "two-step" method of advertising. Request that the reader send you four first-class postage stamps for more information. When they respond, you will send them a brochure, flyer, order form and cover letter so they can place an order for the real product.

E-Z TIP Don't copy ads word-for-word, but use them as a guide to write your own ads. Once you get the hang of it, you'll be writing effective ad copy just as well as the pros.

The best way to learn how to write effective ad copy is to read the ads other people have written.

Advertising in the right publication

Although this may sound like common sense—people will often overlook selectively choosing the right publications in which to run their ads. Instead, they will look for the lowest price for the amount of circulation they receive. Unfortunately, this does not work out. Even though you need to look for good deals that make it easy on your pocketbook, you will be throwing money away if you don't pre-qualify the publication you choose.

Study the publication to see what other people are advertising and how they are advertising it. Contact some of the people who sell items similar to your own with the hope of networking with them.

Once you locate a publication you want to advertise in, give it a try for three months. If you don't get any responses or only a few orders, try another publication. There are thousands of them, and eventually you will hit the right target market that will be interested in what you have to sell.

Don't stop with one publication

You would be surprised how much free publicity you can get just from corresponding, calling and networking with others.

Just because you locate the target market of people who are interested in purchasing your product, there is no reason you can't advertise in more than one publication. In fact, if you don't, your ad will become stale. If the same people continue to see your ad every month, they will probably get tired of looking at it. Besides, if they wanted the product, they would have ordered it by now. Don't tire them out!

Leave your ad running as long as it brings in orders for you, but also advertise in 5, 10, 20 or 50 other publications to generate a steady stream of orders and to reach more people.

Key your ads

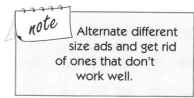

Alternate different size ads and get rid of ones that don't work well.

DEFINITION

Keying your ads means that you place a code of some sort in your address so that when people order something from you, you immediately know where they saw your ad. Record the date you sent the ad and the date you received a checking copy, proving that your ad appeared. Also record the "code" you used so you can immediately identify where it came from. Many beginners in mail order never *key* their ads so they never know where people saw their ads.

If your address is "123 Anytown St.," it could become "123 Anytown St., Suite A" for one publication and "Suite B" for another. The postman will still deliver your mail to "123 Anytown St." Of course, if you live in an apartment complex and there are apartment numbers you could turn "111 Johnson, Apt. A" into "111 Johnson, Apt. A-1" for one publication and "Apt. A-2" for another. Post office box addresses are also simple. Turn "P.O. Box 585" into "P.O. Box 585, Dept. A-1" for one publication and "Dept. A-2" for another.

Keep a record of every name and address of the publishers to which you send an ad.

People will sometimes even change their name on the ad for keying purposes. You might see the name "Harriet's Recipe Book" instead of "Harriet Ranger." Harriet might also use "Harriet's Cookbook" or even "Harriet's Solution to Stress" on her ads relating to these products. Use your own imagination and pretty soon, keying your ads will be a normal part of your life. Be sure to keep track (on your record sheet) of how many responses you receive from each publication. After three months, look over your record sheet and get rid of the publications that didn't do well. After awhile, you'll be able to see where it pays you to advertise your particular product and then you can send in larger ads to those publications. Never stop using this method and you'll never stop getting orders in your mailbox. It's a win-win situation for everybody!

Tabloids versus adsheets

Another question about advertising is whether it's better to advertise in tabloids or adsheets. Many people will sell you information about the "best day" to mail and the "best time" of the year to advertise. They think they have it down to a science and will convince you of their methods. However, there are NO set rules that can be employed by everyone. That's because there are a wide variety of ways to approach various products. If you sell travel services and read a report that told you not to advertise during the summer months, you'd go broke. The summer is the travel industry's biggest money-making season!

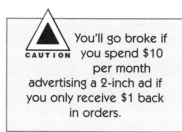 You'll go broke if you spend $10 per month advertising a 2-inch ad if you only receive $1 back in orders.

Don't get hung up on specific statistics made by people who claim to be expert researchers. You are the person in control of your business and you are where the buck stops. Take advantage of your authority and try every angle you can think of until you determine what's best for your company's product and/or service.

Tabloids are a fantastic advertising vehicle and adsheets are too. Sometimes people feel a small 1-inch camera-ready ad gets lost in a tabloid filled with hundreds of them. This may be true in some circumstances and not true in others. Do you look at 1-inch ads in tabloids? Of course you do. You scan the pages and your eye is always directed to one or two on the page. Ask yourself "why" they caught your eye. Was it because the ad was placed in a specific area on the page? Was it because of the headline or the word "free"?

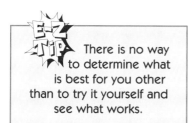 There is no way to determine what is best for you other than to try it yourself and see what works.

Look in the back of the *Globe* or *National Enquirer.* Don't they have page after page of classified ads? If nobody was reading them and responding to them, the advertisers wouldn't be submitting the advertising. So evidently, people DO read classified ads—even if there are hundreds of them. Test the waters and do what works the best for you.

The art of writing classified ads

Writing classified ads is an art, one that can be learned, developed and perfected in a relatively short period of time. Depending on the nature of your business, a well written classified ad can bring in business and subsequent sales.

 As with any business tool (and a classified is a powerful tool), you must first become aware of the effective use of these little business builders, then understand exactly what can be expected of them and what cannot be accomplished.

First, forget the notion of selling merchandise from a classified. Some of the "experts" will tell you that a classified ad can bring cash orders, but this is the exception rather than the general rule. Even in cases where small amounts of cash are received, total results are considerably less than if no money had been requested.

Instead of wondering, speculating and experimenting with your advertising budget, concentrate on offering free information to attract as many interested prospects as possible for what you have to offer.

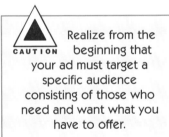

Realize from the beginning that your ad must target a specific audience consisting of those who need and want what you have to offer.

You want inquiries: letters, notes, postcards—anything on which might be scribbled the words, *"Send more information."* When you start receiving them, quickly reply with professionally prepared sales material to tell your story and make your sales pitch. The standard material will consist of a sales letter, descriptive circular or flyer, and a return addressed envelope for convenience.

Zero in on your market

Unlike display advertising which must attract, reach out from the printed page and grab the reader, your classified ad is placed under specific heading according to subject. They are looking for something. You have what they are looking for, or what will help them achieve what they want. Tell them!

No deception, please. What you want are quality names of prospective buyers—not a large quantity of names. It would be easy to promise the moon in your ad, but if you can't deliver it in your follow up advertising, you will not only lose the initial sale, you will have alienated your prospect by deception and they will not be receptive to anything you say in the future.

> *note* Readers interested in your subject will scan the heading in much the same way they would scan the Yellow Pages of the phone directory.

If you're offering something appealing to sportsmen, the heading would probably be SPORTING GOODS. If you're aiming at a specific type of sportsman such as hunters, fishermen, or bowlers, you might find such a heading. In some cases, you can have the publication create a new heading for you for an additional charge. It could be worth the extra cost.

Use words economically

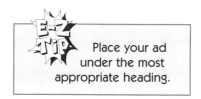

> **E-Z TIP** Place your ad under the most appropriate heading.

The best way to write your ad is to disregard size and cost at first, writing everything on paper that might attract readers. Tell it all. Stress the need for what you have to offer, what it will do for readers, how they will benefit, what they can expect by using your product, and how easy or more pleasant life will be for them.

When you finish writing, you might have a long paragraph or a full page. You will pay by the word, so you will have to be selective in your choice of words in the final ad.

Dos and don'ts of writing classified ads

+ DO WRITE OUT ALL DETAILS in your ad offer. Read it, edit it, and re-write it for a shorter, money-saving effective ad—"think small."

+ DO FOLLOW ALL THE RULES when writing your classified ad. Use these ideas. *Attention—Interest—Desire—Action*

+ DO USE A NAME with each classified ad, including your envelopes.

+ DO BE HONEST with all your classified ad claims.

+ DO IDENTIFY your product.

+ DO WRITE YOUR CLASSIFIED AD simply, clearly, and direct.

+ DO USE WORDS EVERYONE KNOWS and will understand.

+ DO USE A WORD that will benefit a reader.

+ DON'T OVERPRICE your product.

+ DO ADVERTISE FREQUENTLY. Constant exposure creates a familiar offer with better response.

+ DO OFFER A MONEY BACK GUARANTEE in your classified ad, salesletter or circular if possible. An excellent sales technique!

+ DO TEST YOUR AD in 2 or 3 smaller, low cost publications. Code each ad and record results.

+ DO READ PUBLICATIONS that relate to your product. Write for ad rates, paid circulation, discounts and closing dates. Keep records.

✦ DO HAVE ALL YOUR LITERATURE AND PRODUCTS ready for mailing when your ad appears in the publication of your choice. Do not delay in responding.

✦ DO USE THE COPYCAT METHOD. Do what other successful advertisers are doing, only with a slight twist, idea or offer.

✦ DO RUN SEVERAL ADS worded differently. Keep records of results.

✦ DO USE A SHORT BUSINESS NAME. Make it easy to pronounce and remember.

✦ DO NOT CHARGE for sales letters or circulars.

✦ DON'T OVER ADVERTISE. It can be expensive; do it gradually.

✦ DON'T PRETEND YOU KNOW ALL THE ANSWERS. Take time to find out what you need to know.

✦ DON'T TRUST YOUR MEMORY. A thought will leave you as quickly as it came. Always write down a good idea. NOW!

✦ DON'T PLACE YOUR AD in the wrong classification.

✦ DON'T WASTE YOUR MONEY on ad words to amuse or entertain, but use words to persuade, inform and sell your product.

✦ DON'T FORGET THE M.E.D.I.C.S.—Motivation, Enthusiasm, Desire, Image, Creativity, Success!

✦ DON'T GIVE UP. If your ad doesn't pull after a fair exposure, try re-writing it. One or two different words may do the trick.

✦ DON'T SPEND THE PROFITS. Re-invest the money in more continuous advertising.

✦ DON'T FORGET, an ad that offers "FREE DETAILS" means writing a sales letter or circular.

Avoid high typesetting costs and mistakes

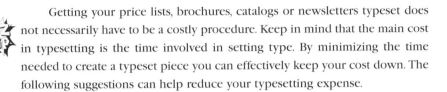

Getting your price lists, brochures, catalogs or newsletters typeset does not necessarily have to be a costly procedure. Keep in mind that the main cost in typesetting is the time involved in setting type. By minimizing the time needed to create a typeset piece you can effectively keep your cost down. The following suggestions can help reduce your typesetting expense.

Have a picture in your mind. Trial and error can be costly. Don't have a typesetter set it one way, then decide a different format would look better. Know what you want the FIRST time around:

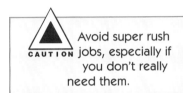

Avoid super rush jobs, especially if you don't really need them.

- Reduce and eliminate author's corrections by thorough proofing and re-proofing.

- Avoid minimum charges by combining small jobs and having them set at the same time.

- Try to use one family of type to save time and money by avoiding font changes. The consistent look is better.

- Give explicit instructions on marking up copy: type styles, column widths/margins.

- With a large job, such as a brochure or annual report, request a style setting proof sheet to get approvals before the entire job is done.

- Avoid lengthy corrections on the phone. You might end up paying for corrections later that could have been avoided if you had done your editing on proof sheets.

- Get the layout finished and approved before having type set. The same goes for copy, of course.

- Avoid the use of "run-arounds" (reducing the width of the copy to make room for a photo in the column, for example). If you do use them, use simple shapes, boxes, or squares.

- Avoid the use of curved or angular type. Type reading left to right on a page (for example, this page) is faster and less expensive to set than copy that is set in a curve or running sideways on the page.

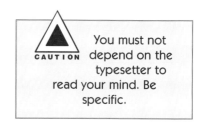

CAUTION You must not depend on the typesetter to read your mind. Be specific.

- The use of unjustified (ragged-edged right margin) text and captions is less expensive than justified because it sets quicker, costing less time.

How to write profitable classified ads

Everybody wants to make more money. In fact, most people would like to hit upon something that makes them fabulously rich! And seemingly, one of the easiest roads to the fulfillment of these dreams of wealth is mail order or, within the professional circles of the business, *direct mail selling*. The only thing is, hardly anyone gives much real thought to the basic ingredient of selling by mail—the writing of profitable classified ads.

So what makes a classified ad good or bad? First of all, it must appeal to the reader and it must say exactly what you want it to say. Secondly, it has to say it in the least possible number of words in order to keep your operating costs within your budget. Finally, it has to produce the desired results—whether inquiries or sales.

Grabbing the reader's attention is your first objective. You must assume the reader is "scanning" the page on which your ad appears in the company of 200 to 300 other classified ads. Therefore, there has to be something about your ad that causes him to stop scanning and look at yours! The first two or three words of your ad are of the utmost importance and deserve your careful consideration. Most surveys show that words or phrases that quickly involve the reader, tend to be the best attention-grabbers. Such words as:

FREE . . . WIN . . . MAKE BIG MONEY

Whatever words you use as attention-grabbers to start your ads, you should bear in mind that they'll be competing with similar attention-grabbers of the other ads on the same page. Therefore, in addition to your lead words, your ad must quickly go on to promise or state further benefits to the reader. In other words, your ad might read something like this: "MAKE BIG MONEY! Easy & Simple. We show you how!"

The next rule of good classified copywriting has to do with the arousal of the reader's desire to get in on your offer. In many instances, this rule is by-passed; this is the real reason that an ad doesn't pull according to the expectations of the advertiser.

note If your mail order business is to succeed, then you *must* acquire the expertise to write classified ads that sell your product or services!

Think about it—you've got your reader's attention; you've told him it's easy and simple; and you're about to ask him to do something. Unless you take the time to make him further "want your offer," your ad is going to only half sell him. He'll compare your ad with the others that grabbed his attention and finally decide upon the one that interests him the most.

Here is the place for you to insert that magic word *"guaranteed"* or some other such word or phrase. So now, you've got an ad that reads: MAKE BIG MONEY! Easy & Simple. Guaranteed!

Now the reader is motivated, and in his mind, he can't lose. You're ready to ask for money. This is the "demand for action" part of your ad. This is the part where you use such words as: "Limited offer—Act now! Write today!"

Putting it all together, your ad might read something like this: "MAKE BIG MONEY! Easy & Simple. Guaranteed! Limited offer. Send $1 to:_____."

These are the ingredients of any good classified ad: Attention—Interest—Desire—Action. Without these four ingredients skillfully integrated into your ad, chances are your ad will just "lie there" and not do anything but cost you money. What we just composed is a basic classified ad. Although such an ad could be placed in any leading publication and would pull a good response, it's known as a "blind ad" and would pull inquiries and responses from a whole spectrum of people reading the publication in which it appeared, from as many "time-wasters" as from bona-fide buyers.

In the language of professional copywriters, you've grabbed the attention of your prospect, and interested him with something that he can do.

Here's an example of the kind of classified ad you might want to use. Using all the rules of basic advertising copywriting, and stating exactly what our product is, our ad reads:

MONEY-MAKER'S SECRETS! How To Write Winning Classified Ads. Simple & easy to learn. Should double or triple your responses. Rush $1 to BC Sales, 10 Main, Anytown, TX 75001.

The point we're making is that you must:

- grab the reader's attention

- interest him with something that appeals to him

- further stimulate the reader with something (catch-phrase) that makes him desire the product or service

- demand that he act immediately

There's no point to being tricky or clever. Just adhere to the basics and your profits will increase accordingly. One of the best ways of learning to write good classified ads is to study the classifieds—try to figure out exactly what they're attempting to sell—and then practice rewriting them according to the rules we just gave you. Whenever you sit down to write a classified, always write it all out—write down everything you want to say—and then go back over it, crossing out words, and refining your phrasing.

The final ingredient of your classified ad is of course, your name and the address to which the reader is to respond—where to send their money or write for further information.

However, because advertising costs are based upon the number of words, or the amount of space your ad uses, the use of some names in classified ads could become quite expensive. If you were to ask our ad respondents to send their money to

> *note* Generally speaking, readers respond more often to ads that include a name than to those showing just initials or an address.

The Research Writers & Publishers Association, or to *Book Business Mart,* or even to *Money Maker's Opportunity Digest,* your advertising costs would be high. Thus, you shorten your name to *Researchers* or *Money-Makers.* The point here is to shorten excessively long names.

The same holds true when listing your post office box number. Shorten it to just plain *Box 40,* or in the case of a rural delivery, shorten it to just *RR1.*

The important thing is to know the rules of profitable classified ad writing, and to follow them. Hold your costs in line.

How to write action-compelling ads that sell

3

Chapter 3

How to write action-compelling ads that sell

The most important aspect of any business is selling the product or service. Without sales, no business can exist for very long.

note All sales begin with some form of advertising.

To build sales, this advertising must be seen or heard by potential buyers and cause them to react to the advertising in some way. The credit for the success, or the blame for the failure, of almost all ads reverts back to the ad itself.

Generally, the "ad writer" wants the reader to do one of the following:

1) Visit the store to see and judge the product, or immediately write a check and send for the merchandise being advertised.

2) Phone for an appointment to hear the full sales presentation, or write for further information.

The bottom line in any ad is quite simple: To make the readers buy the product or service. Any ad that causes readers only to pause in their thinking, to just admire the product, or to simply believe what is written, is not doing its job completely.

The ad writer must know exactly what he wants the reader to do, and any ad that does not elicit the desired action is an absolute waste of time and money.

In order to elicit the desired action from the reader, all ads are written according to a simple "master formula" which is:

note Never forget the basic rule of advertising copywriting: If the ad is not read, it won't stimulate any sales; if it is not seen, it cannot be read; and if it does not command or grab the attention of the reader, it will not be seen!

- Attract the attention of your reader.

- Stimulate your reader's interest in the product.

- Cause your reader to desire the product.

- Demand action from the reader.

Most successful advertising copywriters know these fundamentals backwards and forwards. Whether you know them already or you're just now being exposed to them, your knowledge and practice of these fundamentals will determine the extent of your success as an advertising copywriter.

Classified ads

Classified ads are the way most successful businesses are started. These small, relatively inexpensive ads give the beginner an opportunity to advertise a product or service without losing their shirt if the ad doesn't pull or the people don't break the door down demanding the product. Classified ads are written according to all the advertising rules. The wording is the same as in a larger, more elaborate type of ad, except in condensed form.

To begin learning how to write effective classified ads, clip ten good ads from ten different mail order type publications. Paste each onto a separate sheet of paper.

Analyze each ad. How has the writer attracted your attention? What about the ads keeps your interest? Are you stimulated to want to know more about the product being advertised? Finally, what action must you take? Are all of these points covered in the ad? How strongly are you motivated by each of these ads?

Rate these ads on a scale from one to ten, with ten being the best according to the above formula. Now, just for practice, without clipping the ads, do the same thing with ten different ads from *Sears, Wards,* or the *J.C. Penney's* catalog. In fact, quickly analyze every ad you see from now on, and rate it somewhere on your scale. If you practice this exercise on a regular basis, you'll soon be able to quickly recognize the "power points" of any ad you see, and know whether an ad is good, bad, or otherwise, and what makes it so.

Practice for an hour each day, copy the ads you've rated 8, 9, and 10 exactly as they have been written. This will give you the "feel" of the fundamentals and style necessary to write classified ads.

Your next project will be to select what you consider to be the ten "worst" ads you can find in the classified section. Clip these out and paste them onto a sheet of paper so you can work with them. Read these ads over a couple of times, and then, beside each of them, write a short comment why you think it is bad—lost in the crowd, doesn't attract attention or hold the reader's interest. There's nothing urgent to make the reader yearn to own the product, or no demand for action.

Now, break out those pencils, erasers and scratch paper. Start rewriting these ads to include the missing elements. Each day for the next month, practice writing the ten best ads for an hour, just the way they were originally written. Pick out the ten worst ads, analyze those ads, and then practice rewriting them until they measure up to doing the job they were intended to do.

Once you're satisfied that the ads you've rewritten are perfect, go back into each ad and cross out the words that can be eliminated without detracting from the ad.

EXAMPLE: I'll arrive at 2 o'clock tomorrow afternoon, the 15th. Meet me at Sardi's. All my love, Jim.

EDITED FOR SENDING: Arrive at 2 pm—15th Sardi's. Love, Jim.

CLASSIFIED AD: Save on your food bills! Reduced prices on every shelf in the store! Stock up now while supplies are complete! Come in today, Jerry's Family Supermarket!

EDITED FOR PUBLICATION: Save on Food! Everything bargain priced! Limited supplies—Hurry! Jerry's Markets!

It takes dedication and regular practice, but you can do it. Simply recognize and understand the basic formula—practice reading and writing the good ones and rewriting the bad ones to make them better. Practice, and keep at it, daily until the formula, the idea, and the feel of ad writing becomes second nature to you. This is the ONLY WAY to gain expertise at writing good classified ads.

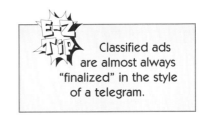

E-Z TIP   Classified ads are almost always "finalized" in the style of a telegram.

Display advertisements

A display or space ad differs from a classified ad because it has a headline, layout, and the style is not telegraphic. However, the fundamentals of writing the display ad are exactly the same as for a classified ad. The basic difference is that you have more room to emphasize the "master formula."

After all, when your ad is surrounded by hundreds of other ads, information, or entertainment, what makes you think anyone is going to see your particular ad?

The truth is, readers are not going to see your ad unless you can "grab" their attention and entice them to read all of what you have to say. Your headline or lead sentence, if no headline is used, has to make it MORE DIFFICULT for your reader to ignore, than to stop and read your ad.

> *note* Most successful copywriters rate the headline and/or the lead sentence of an ad as the most important part.

In successful classified advertising headlines, the first three to five words serve as your headline. They are written as promises, either implied or direct. The first ad below promises to show you how to save money, make money, or attain a desired goal. The second ad is a warning against something undesirable.

EXAMPLE OF A PROMISE: Are You Ready to Become a Millionaire in Just 18 Months?

EXAMPLE OF A WARNING: Do You Make These Mistakes in English?

In both examples, a question is the headline. Headlines that ask a question seem to attract the reader's attention like a moth to a flame. Once the reader has seen the question, he can't keep from reading the rest of the ad to find out the answer. The best headline questions are those that challenge the readers, that involve their self esteem, and do not allow them to dismiss your question with a simple "yes" or "no."

DEFINITION

"You'll be the envy of your friends" is another kind of *reader appeal* to incorporate into your headline whenever appropriate. The appeal has to do with basic psychology. Everyone wants to be well-thought-of and consequently, will read your ad to find out how to gain respect and accolades.

The idea is to shock or shake the readers out of their reverie and cause them to notice your ad. Most of the headlines you see today have a certain sameness with just the words rearranged. The reader may see these headlines with their eyes, but their brain fails to focus on any of them because there is nothing different or out of the ordinary to arrest their attention.

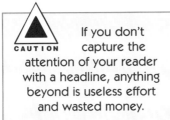

If you don't capture the attention of your reader with a headline, anything beyond is useless effort and wasted money.

EXAMPLE OF A COLLOQUIALISM: Are you Developing a POT BELLY?

Another attention-grabber is the comparative price headline: "Three For only $3, Regularly $3 Each!" Still another of the "tried and proven" headlines is a specific question: "Do You Suffer From These Symptoms?" And of course, if you offer a strong guarantee, you should say so in your headline: "Your Money Refunded, If You Don't Make $100,000 Your First Year."

"How To" headlines have a very strong basic appeal, but in some instances, they are better used as book titles than advertising headlines. Everyone wants to be in on the finer things—which your product or service presumably offers—is another approach with a strong reader appeal. The psychology here is the need to belong to a group . . . complete with status and prestige motivations.

note Wherever and whenever possible, use colloquialisms or words that are not usually found in advertisements.

After all, your ad should be directed to "one" person, and the person reading your ad wants to feel that you're talking to him personally, not everyone who lives on his street.

Personalize, and be specific! You can throw the teachings of your English teachers out the window, and the rules of "third person, singular" or whatever else tends to inhibit your writing. Whenever you sit down to write advertising copy intended to pull the orders, picture yourself in a one-on-one situation and "talk" to your reader just as if you are sitting across from him at your dining room table. Say what you mean, and sell HIM on the product. Be specific, ask him if these are the things that bother him? Are these the things he wants? He is the one you want to buy the product.

The layout you devise for your ad, or the frame you build around it, should also command attention. Either make it so spectacular that it stands out like lobster at a chili dinner, or so uncommonly simple that it catches the reader's eye because of its very simplicity. It's also important not to get cute with a lot of unrelated graphics and artwork. Your ad should convey excitement and movement, but should not tire the eyes or disrupt the flow of the message.

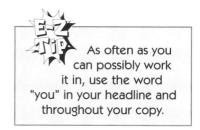

As often as you can possibly work it in, use the word "you" in your headline and throughout your copy.

Any graphics or artwork you use must be relevant to your product, its use and/or the copy you wrote about it. Graphics should not be used as artistic touches, or to create an atmosphere. Any illustrations with your ad should complement the selling of your product, and prove or substantiate specific points in your copy.

Your potential buyer doesn't care in the least how long it's taken you to produce the product, how long you have been in business, nor how many years you spent learning your craft. The buyer wants to know specifically how he's going to benefit from the purchase of the product.

Generally, the buyer's wants will fall into one of the following categories:

• better health

• more comfort

- more money

- more leisure time

- more popularity

- greater beauty

- success and/or security

Once you have your reader's attention, the only way you're going to keep it is by quickly and emphatically telling him what the product will do for him.

Even though you have your reader's attention, you must follow through with a list of the benefits he will gain. In essence, you must reiterate the advantages, comfort, and happiness he will enjoy as you implied in your headline.

Mentally picture your reader. Determine his wants and emotional needs. Put yourself in his shoes, and ask yourself: If I were reading this ad, what are the things that would appeal to me?

Remember, it's not the "safety features" that have sold cars for the past 50 years nor the need for transportation. It has been, and almost certainly always will be, the advertising writer's recognition of the people's wants and emotional needs. Visualize your readers, recognize their wants and satisfy them. Writing good advertising copy is nothing more or less than knowing who your buyers are, recognizing what they want, and telling them how your product will fulfill those wants. Remember this is a vitally important key to writing advertising copy.

The "desire" portion of your ad is where you present the facts about your product; create and justify your readers' conviction, and cause them to demand "a piece of the action."

It's vitally necessary that you present proven facts about your product because surveys show that at least 80% of the people reading your ad, especially those reading it for the first time, will question its authenticity.

The more facts you present in the ad, the more credible your offer. As you write this part of your ad, always remember that the more facts about the product you present, the more product you'll sell. People want facts as reasons and/or excuses for buying a product to justify to themselves and others that they haven't been "taken" by a slick copywriter.

In other words, the "desire" portion of your ad has to build belief and credibility in the mind of your readers. It has to assure them of their good judgment. Furnish evidence of the benefits you promised and afford a "safety net" in case they question their decision to buy.

Once you establish a belief in this manner, logic and reasoning are used to support it. People believe what they want to believe. Your reader wants to believe your ad if he read through this far. It's up to you to support his initial desire.

Study your product and everything about it. Visualize the wants of your prospective buyers—dig up the facts. You'll almost always find plenty of facts to support the buyer's reason for buying.

> **note** Write copy to appeal to your reader's wants and emotional needs.

Here, in the "desire" portion of your ad, is where you use the results of tests, growing sales figures to prove increasing popularity, and "user" testimonials or endorsements. It's also important that you present these facts, test results, sales figures and/or testimonials, from the consumer's point of view, and not that of the manufacturer.

CAUTION Before you end this portion of your ad and go into your demand for action, summarize everything you presented thus far. Draw a mental picture for your potential buyer. Let him imagine owning the product. Induce him to visualize the benefits you promised. Give the reader the keys to seeing himself richer, enjoying luxury, having time to do whatever he'd like to do.

This can be handled in one or two sentences, or spelled out in a paragraph, but it's the absolute ingredient you must include prior to closing the sale. Study all the sales presentations you've ever heard—look at every winning ad—this is the element they all include that actually makes the sale. Remember it, use it, and never try to sell anything without it.

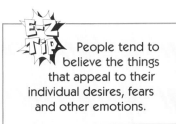

People tend to believe the things that appeal to their individual desires, fears and other emotions.

As Victor Schwab put it so succinctly in his best selling book, *How To Write a Good Advertisement*,

"Every one of the fundamentals in the 'master formula' is necessary. Those people who are 'easy' to sell may perhaps be sold even if some of these factors are left out, but it's wiser to plan advertisement so that it will have a powerful impact upon those who are the 'hardest' to sell. For, unlike face-to-face selling, we cannot in printed advertising come to a 'trial close' in our sales talk—in order to see if those who are easier to sell will welcome the dotted line without further persuasion.

"We must assume that we are talking to the hardest ones—and that the more thoroughly our copy sells both the hard and the easy, the better chance we have against the competition for the consumer's dollar— and also the less dependent we will be upon the usual completely ineffective follow-through on our advertising effort which later takes place at the sales counter itself."

Ask for action! Demand the money!

Lots of ads are beautiful, almost perfectly written, and quite convincing, yet they fail to ask for or demand action from the reader. If you want the reader to have your product, then tell him so and demand that he send money now. Unless you enjoy entertaining your readers with your writing skills, always demand that they complete the sale now, by taking action immediately—by calling a telephone number and ordering, or by signing a check and rushing it to the post office.

Some effective methods to inspire the reader buy:

- All of this can be yours!

- You can start enjoying this new way of life immediately—simply by sending a check for $____!

- Don't put it off, and later wish you had gotten in on the ground floor.

Once you've got the buyer on the hook, land him! Don't let him get away!

- Make out that check now, and be IN on the ground floor!

- Act now, and as an "early bird" buyer, we'll include a big bonus package—absolutely free, simply for acting immediately!

- You win all the way!

- We take all the risk. If you're not satisfied, simply return the product and we'll quickly refund your money.

- Do it now! Get that check on its way to us today, and receive the big bonus package.

- After next week, we won't be able to include the bonus as a part of this fantastic deal, so act now!

- The sooner you act, the more you win!

Beware when offering a reward or bonus—customers may take the bonus, followed by mountains of requests for product refunds. The bonus should be mentioned only casually if you're asking for product orders, but with lots of fanfare when you're seeking inquiries.

Too often the copywriter, in his enthusiasm to pull in a record number of responses, confuses the reader by "forgetting about the product" and devoting the entire "demand for action" space to sending for the bonus. Any reward offered should be closely related to the product, provided the potential buyer acts at once.

Tell your readers that they must act within a certain time limit or lose the bonus, face higher prices, or even face the withdrawal of your offer. This is always a good hook to get action.

note Offering a reward of some kind will almost always stimulate the reader to take action.

Any kind of guarantee you offer helps to produce action from the reader. And, the more liberal you can make your guarantee, the more product orders you'll receive. State the guarantee clearly and simply. Make it so easy to understand that even a child would not misinterpret what you're saying.

The action you want your reader to take should be easy to do, clearly stated, and devoid of complicated or numerous directions to follow.

Picture your readers, comfortable in their favorite easy chairs, idly flipping through a magazine while "half watching" TV. They notice your ad, read through it, and are sold on your product. Now what do they do?

Remember, they are very comfortable—you've "grabbed" their attention, sparked interest, painted a picture of a new kind of satisfaction, and they are ready to buy.

Anything and everything you ask or cause them to do is going to disrupt this aura of comfort and contentment. Whatever they must do had better be simple, quick and easy!

Tell them without any ifs, ands, or buts, what to do—fill out the coupon, include your check for the full amount, and send it in to us today! Be simple and direct. And by all means, your name and address must be on the order form, as well as just above it. People sometimes fill out the coupon, tear it off, seal it in an envelope and don't know where to send it. The easier you make it for them to respond, the more responses you'll get!

Specify a time limit for the reader to respond.

There you have it, a complete short course on how to write ads that will pull more orders for you and sell more of your product. It's important to learn "why" ads are written as they are—to understand and use the "master formula" in your own ads.

By conscientiously studying good advertising copy, and practicing writing ads of your own, you should be able to quickly develop your copywriting abilities to produce order-pulling ads for your own products. Even so, and once you do become proficient in writing ads, you must never stop "noticing" how ads are written, designed, and put together by other people.

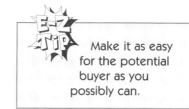

Make it as easy for the potential buyer as you possibly can.

Every time professional ad writers see a good ad, they clip it out and save it. They regularly pull these files of good ads and study them, always analyzing what makes them good, and why they work. You *must* keep yourself up-to-date, aware, and in-the-know about the other guy's innovations, style changes, and methods used to sell his product. On-the-job training, study and practice is what it takes. With a burning ambition to succeed, you can do it too!

Fast answers to common questions

What is the most profitable way to use classifieds?

Classifieds are best used to build a mailing list of qualified readers. Use classifieds to offer a free catalog, booklet or some type of quality report relative to your product line.

What can you sell "directly" from classifieds?

Generally, anything and everything, so long as it doesn't cost more than $5, which is about the most people will pay in response to an offer in the classifieds. These types of ads are great: "Write for further information;" "Send $3, get two for the price of one;" "Dealers wanted, send for product info and a real moneymaking kit!"

What are the best months of the year to advertise?

All twelve months of the year! Responses to your ads during some months will be slower, but by keying your ads according to the month they appear, and carefully tabulating your returns from each keyed ad, you'll see that steady year-round advertising will continue to pull orders for you, regardless of the month.

Are mail order publications good advertising buys?

The least effective are the ad sheets. Most of the ads in these publications are "exchange ads," meaning the publisher of ad sheet "A" runs the ads of publisher "B" without charge, because publisher "B" is running the ads of publisher "A" without charge. The "claimed" circulation figures of these publications are almost always based on "wishes, hopes and wants" while the "true" circulation goes to similar small, part-time mail order dealers.

This is a very poor medium for investing advertising dollars because everyone receiving a copy is a "seller" and nobody is buying. When an ad sheet is received by someone not involved in mail order, it's usually given a cursory glance and then discarded as "junk mail."

The important difference with the tabloids is that they offer the "helpful information" articles for the mail order beginner.

With mail order magazines, it depends on the quality of the publication and its business concepts. Some mail order magazines are nothing more than expanded ad sheets, while others such as *Book Business Mart* strive to help the opportunity seekers with ongoing advice and tips used in the development and growth of wealth building projects.

How can I decide where to advertise my product?

First of all, you have to determine who your buyers might be. Then do a little bit of market research. Talk to friends, neighbors and people at random. Ask them if they would be interested in a product such as yours, and then ask them which publications they read. Next, go to your public library for a listing of the publications of this type from the *Standard Rate & Data Service* catalogs.

Make a list of the addresses, circulation figures, reader demographics and advertising and decide the true costs of your advertising. Decide which is the better buy. Divide the total audited circulation figure into the cost for a one inch ad; $10 per inch with a publication showing 10,000 circulation would be

Tabloid newspapers are slightly better than the ad sheets, but not by much!

10,000 into $10 or 10 cents per thousand. Looking at the advertising rates for *Book Business Mart*, you would divide 42,500 into $15 for an advertising rate of less than 3/10 of 1 cent per thousand. Obviously, your best buy in this case would be *Book Business Mart* because of the lowest price per thousand.

Write and ask for sample copies of the magazines you've tentatively chosen for your advertising. Look over their advertising. Be sure that they don't or won't put your ad in the *"gutter,"* which is the inside column next to the binding. How many other mail order type ads are they carrying? You want to go with a publication that is busy, not one that has only a few ads. The more ads in the publication, the better response the advertisers are getting, or else they wouldn't be investing their money there.

If your responses are small, try a different publication. Then, if your responses are still small, think about rewriting the ad for greater appeal and pulling power. In a great many instances, it's the ad not the publication's pulling power that is at fault!

How info-loading can increase your ad's pulling power

There are many schools of thought on how to write a successful direct-response ad, letter, or brochure. Some say you need to be subtle, some say be harsh, some say be round-about, some say be direct. There is one technique, though, that is coming to the forefront as one of the most successful to employ: info-loading.

The theory of info-loading: you give the customers more information than they would ever want about the product/service, and they'll feel more confident about you and what you offer. Also, the customer who actually reads through it all is the one who's interested enough to buy what you offer.

 Definition: Info-loading is the style of overloading an advertisement with information about your product or service.

Here's how to do it: Say you're planning a 1/4 page display ad in a magazine. Instead of leaving a lot of white space, fill the whole space with text! Load it with as much information as will fit without making it unreadable. To prevent it from looking like a grey blur when the reader's eyes scan through the page, put a bold, black box around the ad, a bold headline, and emphasize important words and phrases with bold print.

You can do the same thing with a mailing. Put together a four-page sales letter loaded with copy, then add a brochure/flyer that re-emphasizes the important points in even greater detail.

A few cautions with this technique: First, make sure you actually have something to say! We are so conditioned to being economical with our words in advertising that it'll be hard to info-load without feeling repetitious. Instead of rambling on about features, tell customers every single benefit they'll get from your product/service. BENEFIT is the important word. Give info-loading a try. Depending on your audience and what you're trying to sell, you may find that info-loading can load more sales into your bank account!

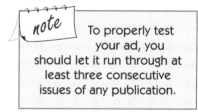 *note* To properly test your ad, you should let it run through at least three consecutive issues of any publication.

100 words with sales appeal:

Add sales punch to describe your merchandise or sales offer—use one or more of the following words. They were selected from successful ads for your convenience in preparing copy:

Absolutely	Amazing	Approved	Attractive
Authentic	Bargain	Beautiful	Better
Big	Colorful	Colossal	Complete
Confidential	Crammed	Delivered	Direct
Discount	Easily Endorsed	Enormous	Excellent
Exciting	Exclusive	Expert	Famous
Fascinating	Fortune	Full	Genuine
Gift	Gigantic	Greatest	Guaranteed
Helpful	Highest	Huge	Immediately
Improved	Informative	Instructive	Interesting
Largest	Latest	Lavishly	Liberal
Lifetime	Limited	Lowest	Magic
Mammoth	Miracle	Noted	Odd
Outstanding	Personalized	Popular	Powerful
Practical	Professional	Profitable	Profusely
Proven	Quality	Quickly	Rare
Reduced	Refundable	Remarkable	Reliable
Revealing	Revolutionary	Scarce	Secrets
Security	Selected	Sensational	Simplified
Sizable	Special	Startling	Strange
Strong	Sturdy	Successful	Superior
Surprise	Terrific	Tested	Tremendous
Unconditional	Unique	Unlimited	Unparalleled
Unsurpassed	Unusual	Useful	Valuable
Wealth	Weird	Wonderful	

70 phrases that stimulate action

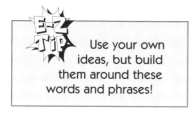

Use your own ideas, but build them around these words and phrases!

Close your ad with an action-getting phrase. Give the reader something to write or do. Here are 70 suggestions for ways to get action. Study them. They will help you prepare your copy for better results.

Act now!

All sent free to introduce

Free

Bargain lists sent free

Booklet free!

Complete details free

Dealers write for prices

Details free!

Everything supplied!

Extra for promptness

Folder free!

Free booklet explains

Free selling kit

Free with approvals

Get facts that help

Get your copy now!

Gifts with purchases

Interesting details free

It's Free!

Literature free

Money making facts free

Offer limited!

Only 10 cents to introduce

Order Now!

Send your name

Amazing literature

Ask for free folder

Be first to qualify

Catalog included free

Current list free

Description sent free

Dime brings details

Exciting details free

First lesson, 25 cents

For literature, write:

Free plans tell how

Free wholesale plan

Full particulars free

Get started today!

Get yours wholesale

Illustrated lists free

Investigate today

Act Now!

Mail material to:

No obligation! Write!

Send today

Order direct from:

Don't Delay!

Particulars free

Request free literature

Rush name for details

Sample details free

See before you buy

Send for it today

Send post card today

Send today

Stamp brings details

Test lesson free

Valuable details free

Write us first!

15 cent stamp for details

32-page catalog free

Postcard brings details

Revealing booklet free

Sales kit furnished

Samples sent on trial

Send for free details

Send no money

Send 15 cents for mailing

Send your want lists

Stamped envelope brings

Unique sample offer

Write for free booklet free

Yours for the asking

$1 brings complete . . .

The 100 most threatening spelling words

occasion	recommend	occurred	principal
equipped	accommodate	disappoint	possession
privilege	proceed	inconvenience	accept
business	necessary	personal	receive
reference	separate	their	whether
questionnaire	criticism	description	effect
extension	judgment	quantity	similar
undoubtedly	height	immediately	stationery
foreign	fourth	government	omitted
weather	personnel	existence	analysis
across	appearance	loose	pamphlet
practical	preferred	unnecessary	affect
attendance	incidentally	apparent	calendar
professor	strictly	principle	already
coming	its	oblige	opportunity

original	paid	probably	referring
referred	there	too	writing
among	arrangement	practically	convenient
canceled	really	using	beginning
especially	volume	committee	confident
difference	endeavor	explanation	except
sincerely	experience	benefited	conscientious
eligible	acquaintance	controversy	exceed
laboratory	omission	procedure	acknowledgment
Wednesday	guarantee	February	schedule

The key is to combine your words. For example, "The Magic Mammoth Miracle;" "The Three "M" Program." This has already caught the attention and interest of your prospect! Now . . . for example say: "The Money Making Facts are FREE! Merely enclose your SASE or $$." Fill in with a few details, and you have a tremendous pulling ad. Always remember, your follow-up material must be just as interesting to get the orders.

Ways to use the word "free" in your ads

The word "FREE" is still the most powerful . . . the most often used word in advertising today! If you have anything to offer FREE to others, you can use this powerful word. It pulls orders better than any other word. Here's some ways to use it:

- "ONE thing FREE when you buy another!"—This can be the way to get people to order from you! A second one is, "FREE, with the purchase of the first!"

- "Buy 2—get the third FREE!"—This can be used to get more and larger orders! Giving away ONE, with the purchase of two others!

- "Fourth FREE, with purchase of three!"—Tire stores and publishers offer a 4th FREE, when you buy three others at regular price.

- "FREE Trial Size!"—Give away one that's smaller than usual, hoping that people will LIKE what you give them, and want to buy more.

- "FREE Bedframe, with purchase of a king-size set!"—Lots of mattress stores use this type of ad. Offering some sort of "premium" FREE with purchase.

- "FREE Introductory Class!"—This usually is offered with purchase of a computer; microwave oven, etc.

- "Use it FREE for 30 days!"—Allow people to use something; to use your product or service, FREE, for a limited time (enticing them to order).

- "FREE Service with each purchase!"—This is used often by pizza companies, and cleaning services. Free delivery; free folding, etc.

- "FREE Interest for 3 months!"—Many loan companies and others offer this to entice customers to buy from them. It's delaying something for a time.

- "Fast service, or it's FREE!" "It's Hot, or it's Free!"—7-11 offers hot coffee, Denny's says "10 Minutes, or it's FREE!" Customers come to see!

- "2nd Topping is FREE, with purchase of a Large Pizza!"—That about says it all.

- "FREE Details!"—This is used by a lot of advertisers, who sell products by mail. Let them know you'll send information FREE, just to write and ask.

- "Buy 2 ads, get a 3rd (or 4th) FREE!"—This is another way to get long-term advertisers. They get FREE ads, with every 3rd or 4th they buy.

- "FREE Commission Circulars!"—Many prime sources are willing to offer you FREE circulars (some for postage) to obtain dealers.

- "FREE Typesetting, with purchase of an ad!"—Publishers offer this free service to obtain new advertisers.

- "FREE Catalog!"—Many companies send out catalogs free to anyone who writes and asks for one.

- "FREE Sample Copy!"—Some companies will to send you ONE FREE to entice you to buy more later.

How to code your ads

A great many firms sell reports on how to code your advertising for $3 or more, when it's nothing you can't learn with a little study of a few mail order publications.

DEFINITION

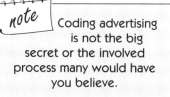
note Coding advertising is not the big secret or the involved process many would have you believe.

Coding advertisements is simply a means of determining where your orders come from and, in cases where you don't use coupons or separate order forms for several different products, a method of double checking on what the customer actually requested.

For the purpose of demonstration, let's assume you have a company called JONDO COMPANY, your name is JOHN DOE, and you market publications by PRINTCO and PUB-GUYS. You decide to run ads for different products in three publications and teaser ads for your catalogs in two others, one for each publisher's catalog. Coding the latter two is easy.

For simplicity, where you put the name and address of the company when offering Printco's catalog, mark the name as PC JONDO, ADDRESS, ZIP CODE. When the envelope arrives and no indication is given of what was requested, you can tell at a glance what was requested.

Now Printco and Pub-Guys sound and look alike, so for the second ad, mark it JONDO-PG. If you're advertising the same catalog in three different magazines, use different codes for each to see which one gives you the best response, for example JONDO-PG, JOHN DOE PG AND P.G. JOHN. You can easily separate them as you receive them.

The permutations are endless: P.G. DOE, P. DOE, G. DOE, DPG, JPG, JDPG, and if that's not enough, code the address, perhaps BOX 99, DEPT. PG, BOX 99-PG, BOX 99 DESK PG, BOX PG-99, and so on.

The person ordering wants to be sure you get his request and almost always faithfully reproduces whatever is listed as the correct address right down to the last comma. PG is the

note You can never run out of ways to code.

obvious code for PUB-GUYS, but you could use an arbitrary number code chosen by you and in fact, number codes are invaluable codes for making dates on the ads, to see how many trickle-in orders you get long after the ad stops running, and what months and season are most productive for selling your products.

Date coding involves using numbers in sequence to indicate magazine issue number, sequence number, or date published.

This coding is virtually essential in later campaigns. Once you've got a fair-sized mailing list, it will be far easier to use advertising codes to indicate their interests than to keep a complete ledger of every person and what they purchased. It also makes computer entry a snap, especially with a good filing program.

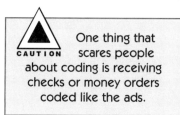

One thing that scares people about coding is receiving checks or money orders coded like the ads.

People become somewhat afraid that they won't be able to deposit their checks because their account is registered to JONDO, not JDPG or whatever. Have no fear. Your company will be registered to your mailing address. By showing the clerk a copy of the advertisement with the address, there will be little doubt as to who should rightfully receive the money, and your checks or money orders will clear like clockwork. If by chance you do encounter a bank that won't accommodate this requirement, bank somewhere else where they understand the workings of mail marketers.

Position your ads to pull

4

Chapter 4

Position your ads to pull

Classified advertising has always been, and will continue to be, the favorite method for mail order "pros" to advertise. Almost all mail order pros started with these tiny inexpensive ads since they represent the best cost-effective way to reach millions of people.

Two basic methods

Two basic methods are used with classified advertising:

1) Place an ad offering FREE literature, and then send your literature to all inquiries. A free offer will always out-pull an ad that requests money, but your overall profits may be larger since you will generate more inquiries. This method is excellent when you are also collecting "Opportunity Seeker" names that you can rent. You should be able to generate fresh national leads for 20 cents to $1 using this method.

2) Offer a report for $2 or $3 and then send other offers with your orders. This eliminates the "Opportunity Seeker" who never buys anything, and your operation is much cleaner and void of "busy" work.

Over 200 listed publications

The following is a list of over 200 magazines that offer classified advertising. The first group of magazines often outpull other magazines for opportunity offers. The second group was selected from thousands of other magazines because:

- they offer classified advertising

- they are the least expensive (word cost/circulation ratio).

Cost/circulation ratios

DEFINITION

This may seem like an expensive ad, but the cost to get your 10-word ad to 1,000 people is only ($.0023 x 10) = $.023! That's right—two cents! For every 1,000 people! Therefore, learn to evaluate the *circulation/cost ratio* since this will tell you the relative cost that is important. As a further example, consider advertising in *"Hounds And Hunting."* Here the cost for a word is only 22 cents. Good deal? NO! In this case your word cost per 1,000 is $.0227. Therefore, your cost to place a 10 word ad per 1,000 people is ($.0227 x 10) = $.227! That's over 10 times more expensive than the *National Enquirer*! However, if you were selling something for hunting, it might actually pull better than *National Enquirer*.

Ask for the rate card

Before you place an ad, write to the magazine and ask for their "Rate Card" for both classified ads and space advertising. You will normally receive a large package containing a sample publication, advertising rates, schedules and discounts offered for multiple insertions placed for sequential publication dates.

These publications have produced excellent results for opportunity offers:

MAGAZINE NAME	CIRCULATION	FREQUENCY
Black Enterprise 130 Fifth Avenue New York, NY 10011	240,000	Monthly
Book Business Mart Premier Publishers, P.O. Box 330309 Fort Worth, TX 76163-0309	50,000	3 times/yr
Capper's Stauffer's Magazine Group 1503 S.W. 42nd St Topeka, KS 66609-1265	353,422	26 times/yr
Classified, Inc. 100 E. Ohio Street, Suite 632 Chicago, IL 60611	25,000,000+	Monthly
Crafts Magazine P.O. Box 1790 Peoria, IL 61656	1,000,000	Monthly
Crafts 'N Things 701 Lee St. #1000 Des Plaines, IL 60016	287,828	8 times/yr
Entrepreneur P.O. Box 570 Clearwater, FL 34617-0570	1,700,000	Monthly

Family Handyman, The 28 W. 23rd Street New York, NY 10010	1,000,000	10 times/yr
Fate 200,000 Llewellyn Publications, Box 64383 St. Paul, MN 55164	Monthly	
Field & Stream Two Park Avenue New York, NY 10016-5695	2,000,000	Monthly
Globe Group P.O. Box 21 Rouses Point, NY 12979-0021	3,000,000	Weekly
Grier's Almanac P.O. Box 888281 Atlanta, GA 30356	3,011,680	Annually
Grit Stauffer's Magazine Group 1503 S.W. 42nd Street Topeka, KS 66609-1265	330,496	10 times/yr
Home Mechanix 2 Park Ave., New York, Ny 10016	1,003,244	Monthly
Income Opportunities 1500 Broadway, Suite 600 New York, NY 10019	400,000	Monthly
Mail Profits P.O. Box 4785 Lincoln, NE 68504	15,000	6 times/yr

Money Making Opportunities 11071 Ventura Boulevard Studio City, CA 91604	222,000	8 times/yr
National Enquirer P.O. Box 10178 Clearwater, FL 34617	3,500,000	Weekly
NC. Magazine 38 Commercial Wharf Boston, MA 02110-3883	647,211	Monthly
Opportunity & Income Plus 73 Spring Street, #303 New York, NY 10012	250,000	Monthly
Popular Science 2 Park Avenue New York, NY 10016	1,861,155	Monthly
Popular Mechanics 224 West 57th Street New York, NY 10019	1,633,210	Monthly
Spare Time Magazine 5810 W. Oklahoma Avenue Milwaukee, WI 53219	301,000	9 times/yr
The Star P.O. Box 1510 Clearwater, FL 34617	2,900,000	Weekly
Success P.O. Box 570 Clearwater, FL 34617-0570	1,200,000	10 times/yr

Workbench 700 West 47th St., Suite 310 Kansas City, MO 64112	1,025,000	6 times/yr
The Workbasket 700 West 47th St., Suite 310 Kansas City, MO 64112	2,726,000	6 times/yr

This group represents more good magazines with low cost/circulation ratios

MAGAZINE NAME	CIRCULATION	FREQUENCY
Americana 29 W. 38th Street New York, NY 10018	325,186	Monthly
American Cage-Bird Mag. One Glamore Court Smithtown, NY 11787	40,000	Monthly
American Handgunner Magazine Publishers Development 591 Camino de la Reina, Ste. 200 San Diego, CA 92108	179,751	6 times/yr
American Legion Magazine P.O. Box 1055 Indianapolis, IN 46206	3,004,913	Monthly
American Business 1775 Broadway New York, NY 10019	104,772	Monthly

American Film 3 E. 54th Street New York, NY 10022	133,232	Monthly
American Motorcyclist 33 Collegeview Road Westerville, OH 43081	176,169	Monthly
American Collector's Journal P.O. Box 407 Kewanee, Il 61443	50,926	Bi-Monthly
Antique Monthly P.O. Drw. 2 Tuscaloosa, AL 35402	66,243	Monthly
American Photographer 1515 Broadway New York, NY 10036	254,107	Monthly
Antique Trader Weekly P.O. Box 1050 Dubuque, IA 52001	190,000	Weekly
The American Rifleman 470 Spring Park Place Herndon, VA 22070	1,372,371	Monthly
American Hunter, The 470 Spring Park Place Herndon, VA 22070	1,359,643	Monthly
Archaeology 15 Park Row New York, NY 10038	105,146	Monthly

Archery 319 Barry Ave., Suite 101 Wayzata, MN 55391	113,023	Monthly
Auto Racing Digest Trump Card Marketing 222 Cedar Lane Teaneck, NJ 07666	44,124	Monthly
Bassmaster One Bell Road Montgomery, AL 36117	530,757	Monthly
The BackStretch 19363 James Couzens Hwy Detroit, MI 48235	25,380	Monthly
Basketball Digest Trump Card Marketing, 222 Cedar Lane Teaneck, NJ 07666	104,238	8 times/yr
Bird Talk P.O. Box 57900, 2401 Beverly Blvd. Los Angeles, CA 90057-0900	123,134	Monthly
Blums Farmer's Almanac 3301 Healy Dr. S.W. Winston-Salem, NC 27103	100,000	Annually
Baseball Digest Trump Card Marketing, 222 Cedar Lane Teaneck, NJ 07666	297,490	Monthly

B'nai B'rith Jewish Monthly 823 United Nations Plaza New York, NY 10017	171,457	Monthly
Boating 1515 Broadway New York, NY 10036	188,057	Monthly
Body, Mind & Spirit P.O. Box 701 Providence, RI 02401	152,000	Monthly
Backpacker 1515 Broadway New York, NY 10036	172,111	Monthly
Bowling Digest Trump Card Marketing 222 Cedar Lane Teaneck, NJ 07666	104,159	Monthly
Bestways P.O. Box 2028 Carson City, NV 89702	161,815	Monthly
Bowling 5301 South 76th Street Greendale, WI 53129-0500	131,351	6 times/yr
Banana Republic Trips Mag. One Harrison Street San Francisco, CA 94105	300,000	Monthly
Camping & RV Magazine P.O. Box 337 Iola, WI 54945	20,000	Monthly

The Christian Herald 40 Overlook Drive Chappaqua, NY 10514	142,376	Monthly
Corvette Fever Petersen Publishing Co. 3816 Industry Boulevard Lakeland, FL 33811		Monthly
Country Music City News 50 Music Square West, 6th Floor Nashville, TN 37203-3246	500,000	Monthly
California Senior Citizens 4805 Alta Canyada Road La Canada, CA 91011	69,000	Monthly
Canoe P.O. Box 3146 Kirkland, WA 98083	64,060	Monthly
Cat Fancy 2401 Beverly Boulevard Los Angeles, CA 90057	237,528	Monthly
Cats Magazine 445 Merrimac Drive Port Orange, FL 32019	129,332	Monthly
Car and Driver 1515 Broadway New York, NY 10036	900,691	Monthly
Cars and Parts P.O. Box 482, 911 Vandermark Rd. Sidney, OH 45365	106,111	Monthly

Car Collector/Car Classics P.O. Box 28571 Atlanta, GA 30328	31,318	Monthly
Circus 3 West 18th Street New York, NY 10011	281,842	Monthly
Changing Times 1729 H St. N.W, Washington, DC 20006	1,372,867	Monthly
Classic Toy Trains 11027 North Seventh St. Milwaukee, WI 53233	10,000	Monthly
Collectors Mart P.O. Box 12830 Wichita, KS 67277	86,623	6 times/yr
Craft Art Needlework Digest P.O. Box 584 Lake Forest, IL 60045	101,189	Bimonthly
Crochet World House of White Birches 306 East Parr Rd Berne, IN 46711	72,300	6 times/yr
Cycle 1515 Broadway New York, NY 10036	373,398	Monthly
Cycle News 2201 Cherry Ave. Long Beach, CA 90806	60,700	Monthly

Dog Fancy Bowtie Press, P.O. Box 6050 Mission Viego, CA 92690	135,320	Monthly
Darkroom Photography 9021 Melrose Ave. Los Angeles, CA 90069	70,508	8 times/yr
Dirt Bike 10600 Sepulveda Blvd. Mission Hills, CA 91345	131,930	Monthly
Dirt Wheels 10600 Sepulveda Blvd. Mission Hills, CA 91345	88,632	Monthly
Dune Buggies & Hot VW's 2950-A7 Airway Ave. Costa Mesa, CA 92626	107,302	Monthly
Dog World 29 North Wacker Dr. Chicago, IL 60606	64,732	Monthly
Easyriders 28210 Dorothy Dr. Agoura Hills, CA 91301	356,590	Monthly
The Ensign P.O. Box 31664 Raleigh, NC 27622	54,534	Monthly
Equus 656 Quince Orchard Rd. Gaithersburg, MD 20878	138,011	Monthly

Farm Journal 230 W. Washington Sq Philadelphia, PA 19106-3599	730,145	13 times/yr
The Farmer 1999 Shepard Rd. St. Paul, MN 55116	118,459	21 times/yr
Finescale Modelier 1027 N. 7th Street Milwaukee, WI 53233	77,748	Bimonthly
Family Motor Coach Association 8291 Clough Pike Cincinnati, OH 45244	98,000	Monthly
Flower and Garden 700 West 47th. St., Suite 310 Kansas City, MO 64112	4,171,000	6 times/yr
Full Cry Gault Publications, P.O. Box 10 Boody, IL 62514	33,955	Monthly
Fur-Fish-Fame 2878 E. Main Street Columbus, OH 43209	172,847	Monthly
Fishing World 700 West 47th St., Suite 310 Kansas City, MO 64112	341,215	6 times/yr
Football Digest Trump Card Marketing 222 Cedar Lane Teaneck, NJ 07666	203,182	10 times/yr

Flying Models Box 700 Newtown, NJ 07860	27,073	Monthly
Golf 380 Madison Avenue New York, NY 10017	912,157	Monthly
Golf Digest 5520 Park Avenue Trumbull, CT 06611	1,239,100	Monthly
Guns & Ammo 8490 Sunset Boulvard Los Angeles, CA 90063	521,638	Monthly
Guns Magazine Publisher's Development 591 Camino de la Reina, Ste. 200 San Diego, CA 92108	205,619	Monthly
Good Old Days House of White Birches, 306 East Parr Road Berne, IN 46711	72,500	Monthly
Gun Dog 1901 Bell Ave., Suite 4 Des Moines, IA 50315	62,973	Bimonthly
Gun Week Box 488 Station C Buffalo, NY 14209	20,000+	Weekly

Guitar World 1115 Broadway New York, NY 10010	128,823	Monthly
Hemmings Motor News P.O. Box 256 Rt 9, West Boulevard Bennington, VT 05201	261,551	Monthly
Hispanic Business 360 S. Hope Ave., Suite C. Santa Barbara, CA 93105	107,875	Monthly
Hounds and Hunting Box 372 Bradford, PA 16701	9,697	Monthly
Knitting Digest House of White Birches 306 East Parr Rd. Berne, IN 46711	25,600	6 times/yr
Ladies Birthday Alman., The 1715 W. 38th Street Chattanooga, TN 37409	3,803,450	Annually
Lapidary Journal P.O. Box 80937 San Diego, CA 92138	35,982	Monthly
Linn's Stamp News P.O. Box 29 Sidney, OH 45365	74,082	Weekly
Model Railroader 1027 N. 7th Street Milwaukee, WI 53233	181,683	Monthly

Old Farmers Almanac, The P.O. Box 520, Main Street Dublin, NH 03444	4,400,000	Annually
Railfan and Railroad Carsten's Publications, Inc. P.O. Box 700, Newton, NJ 07860	144,216	Monthly
Sports Collectors Digest 700 East State Street Iola, WI 54990	43,361	Weekly
Muscle Car Review Petersen Publishing Co. 3816 Industry Boulevard Lakeland, FL 33811	71,235	10 times/yr
Quiltworld House of White Birches 306 East Parr Rd. Berne, IN 46711	71,000	6 times/yr
Sew News P.O. Box 1790, News Plaza Peoria, IL 61656	235,000	Monthly
Shooting Times News Plaza, P.O. Box 1790 Peoria, IL 61656	196,441	Monthly
National History 488 Madison Avenue New York, NY 10022	511,463	Monthly

Trains 1027 N. 7th Street Milwaukee, WI 53233	91,749	Monthly
QST 225 Main Street Newington, CT 06111	161,442	Monthly
Railroad Model Craftsman Carsten's Publications, Inc. P.O. Box 700, Newton, NJ 07860	72,315	Monthly
Powerboat 15917 Strathern Street Van Nuys, CA 91406	83,224	11 times/yr
Saturday Evening Post 1100 Waterway Boulevard Indianapolis, IN 46202	500,000	6 times/yr
Successful Farming Locust at 17th Des Moines, IA 50336	575,686	14 times/yr
Hunting 8490 Sunset Boulevard Los Angeles, CA 90069	311,715	Monthly
Michigan Out-Of-Doors 2101 Wood Street Lansing, MI 48912	101,066	Monthly

The Rotarian 1560 Sherman Avenue Evanston, IL 60201	510,000	Monthly
Organic Gardening 33 E. Minor Street Emmanus, PA 18098	1,188,335	Monthly
Motor Trend 8490 Sunset Boulevard Los Angeles, CA 90069	738,964	Monthly
Soldiers of Fortune P.O. Box 693 Boulder, CO 80306	105,000	Monthly
W.C.—Cross Stitch 306 East Parr Rd Berne, IN 46711	72,851	Bimonthly
Our Sunday Visitor 200 Noll Plaza Huntington, IN 46750	115,000	Weekly
W.C.—Home Cooking 306 East Parr Road Berne, IN 46711	68,265	Monthly
Pro-rodeo 101 Pro-rodeo Dr. Colorado Springs, CO 80919	26,567	Bi-weekly
Modern Photography 825 Seventh Avenue New York, NY 10019	650,386	Monthly

The Highlander P.O. Box 397 Barrington, IL 60011	38,000	7 times /yr
National Speed Sport News P.O. Box 608 79, Chestnut Street Ridgewood, NJ 07451-0608	75,000	Weekly
National Review 150 E. 35 Street New York, NY 10016	240,000	25 times/yr
Teddy Bear and Friends 900 Fredrick Street Cumberland, MD 21502	60,743	6 times/yr
Shutterbug P.O. Box F Titusville, FL 32781	90,000	Monthly
High Fidelity 825 7th Avenue New York, NY 10019	300,172	Monthly
Skiing 1515 Broadway New York, NY 10036	440,370	7 times/yr
Soundings 33 Pratt Street Essex, CT 06426	105,606	Monthly
Motorcyclist 8490 Sunset Boulevard Los Angeles, CA 90069	209,757	Monthly

Horoscope 245 Park Avenue New York, NY 10167	104,200	Monthly
Practical Homeowner 33 E. Minor Street Emmaus, PA 18048	708,504	9 times/yr
Pipe Smoker P.O. Box 22085 Chattanooga, TN 37422	25,000	Monthly
Today's Chicago Woman 200 West Superior, #400 Chicago, IL 60610	125,000	Monthly
Lottery Player's Magazine 321 New Albany Road Moorestown, NJ 08057	180,127	Monthly
The Quarter Horse Journal 2701 I-40 East, P.O. Box 200 Amarillo, TX 79168	67,664	Monthly
W.C—Country Needlecraft 306 East Parr Road Berne, IN 46711	44,508	Monthly
Modern Drummer 870 Pomton Avenue Cedar Grove, NJ 07009	78,400	Monthly
International Travel News 2120 28th Street Sacramento, CA 95818	26,109	Monthly

Kiwanis 3636 Woodview Trace Indianapolis, IN 46268	279,249	Monthly
Power and Motoryacht 1234 Summer Street Stamford, CT 06905	135,319	Monthly
Modern Electronics 76 N. Broadway Hicksville, NY 11801	75,241	Monthly
Sail 100 First Avenue Charlestown, MA 02129	175,212	Monthly
The Lutheran 426 S. Fifth Avenue Minneapolis, MN 55448	1,083,181	Monthly
The Horse Trader P.O. Box 728 Middlefield, OH 44062	28,370	Monthly
Passenger Train Journal P.O. Box 6128 Glendale, CA 91205	16,151	Monthly
Runner's World 33 E. Minor Street Emmaus, PA 18049	451,512	Monthly
The Log P.O. Box 89309 San Diego, CA 92318	46,960	Monthly

Harvard Magazine 7 Ware Street Cambridge, MA 02138	186,677	Monthly
Horse Illustrated 25025 I-45 North, Suite 390 Spring, TX 77380	135,609	Monthly
Trailer Boats 20700 Belshaw Avenue Carson, CA 90746	72,501	Monthly
Skip P.O. Box 404 Bala Cynwyd, PA 19004	35,400	Monthly
Trailblazer 15375 S.E. 30th Place Bellevue, WA 98007	94,572	Monthly
Saltwater Sportsman 186 Lincoln Street Boston, MA 02111	128,521	Monthly
Midwest Outdoors 111 Shore Drive Burr Ridge, IL 60521	37,773	Monthly
Southern Outdoors P.O. Box 17915 Montgomery, AL 36141	288,963	Monthly
The Western Horseman 3850 N. Nevada Avenue Colorado Springs, CO 80933	162,369	Monthly

Mother Jones 1633 Misson Street San Francisco, CA 94103	183,864	Monthly
The Owner Builder 1516 Fifth Street Berkeley, CA 94710	66,150	Monthly
Pennsylvania Sportsman P.O. Box 5196 Harrisburg, PA 17110	65,490	Monthly
Small Boat Journal Box 400 Bennington, VT 05201	57,103	Monthly
True West P.O. Box 2107 Stillwater, OK 74076	32,939	Monthly
Jazz Times 8055 13th St., Suite 301 Silver Springs, MD 20910	49,237	Monthly
Tours & Resorts 990 Grove Street Evanston, IL 60201	194,716	Monthly
Hockey Digest Trump Card Marketing 222 Cedar Lane, Teaneck, NJ 07666	103,506	Monthly
The Nation 72 5th Avenue New York, NY 10011	79,978	Monthly

Motor Boating and Sailing 224 W. 57th Street New York, NY 10019	141,463	Monthly
National Lampoon 155 Avenue of the Americas New York, NY 10013	250,002	Monthly
Total Health 6001 Topanga Canyon Road Woodland Hills, CA 91367	71,010	Monthly
Horticulture 20 Park Plaza, Suite 1220 Boston, MA 02116	178,508	Monthly
New Age 342 Western Avenue Brighton, MA 02135	151,730	Monthly
N.J. Hunting and Fishing P.O. Box 100 Somerdale, NJ 08083	15,000	Monthly
Outdoor America 1701 N. Ft. Meyer Drive Arlington, VA 22209	43,422	Monthly
Sport Fishing 809 South Orlando Avenue Winter Park, FL 32789	109,384	Monthly

Old West P.O. Box 2107 Stillwater, OK 74076	28,385	Monthly
Treasure 6745 Adobe Road 29 Palms, CA 92277	22,679	Monthly
Petersen's Photo Magazine 8490 Sunset Boulevard Los Angeles, CA 90069	283,010	Monthly
Fine Woodworking P.O. Box 355 Newtown, CT 06470	296,773	Monthly
Old House Journal 69th & Seventh Avenue Brooklyn, NY 11217	97,948	6 times/yr
Snowmobile 319 Barry Ave.S., Suite 101 Wayzata, MN 55391	419,478	Monthly
Lost Treasure P.O. Box 937 Bixby, OK 74008	41,423	Monthly
The N.Y. Review of Books 250 E. 57th Street New York, NY 10107	114,234	Monthly
Pure-Bred Dogs Amer. Kennel 51 Madison Avenue New York, NY 10010	53,950	Monthly

Saturday Review 214 Massachusetts Avenue, N.E. Washington, DC 20002	200,000	Monthly
Human Events 422 First St. S.E., Washington, DC 20037	36,695	Monthly
Soccer Digest Trump Card Marketing 222 Cedar Lane Teaneck, NJ 07666	27,929	Monthly
High Technology Business 214 Lewis Wharf Boston, MA 02110	203,678	Monthly
Motorcross Action 10600 Sepulveda Boulevard Mission Hills, CA 91345	92,257	Monthly
Threads P.O. Box 355/63, S. Main Street Newtown, CT 06470	125,913	Monthly
UTNE Reader 2732 West 43rd Street Minneapolis, MN 55410	67,449	Monthly
Practical Horseman Gum Tree Corner Unionville, PA 19375	55,752	Monthly
Miniature Collector 170 5th Avenue New York, NY 10010	23,602	Quarterly

The Magazine Antiques 980 Madison Avenue New York, NY 10021	60,578	Monthly
Selling P.O. Box 570 Clearwater, FL 34617-9862	100,000	Quarterly
Mustang Monthly Petersen Publishing Co. 3816 Industry Boulevard Lakeland, FL 33811		Monthly
Super Ford Petersen Publishing Co. 3816 Industry Boulevard Lakeland, FL 33811		Monthly
Mopar Muscle Petersen Publishing Co. 3816 Industry Boulevard Lakeland, FL 33811		6 times/yr
UCLA Monthly 1633 Westwood Blvd., Ste 110 Los Angeles, CA 90024	186,000	Monthly
Video Marketplace 990 Grove Street Evanston, IL 60201	140,000	Monthly
Video 460 W. 34th Street New York, NY 10001	407,050	Monthly

Video Review 902 Broadway New York, NY 10010	450,001	Monthly
Western Boatman 20700 Belshaw Avenue Carson, CA 90746	23,961	Monthly
Winning! Newsletter 5300 City Plex Tower Jenks, OK 74037-5300	100,000	Monthly
Woodenboat P.O. Box 78 Brooklyn, ME 04616	103,180	Monthly
Writer's Digest 1507 Dana Avenue Cincinnati,OH 45207	220,196	Monthly
Women's Circle House of White Birches 306 East Parr, Road Berne, IN 46711	49,100	6 times/yr
Women's Household House of White Birches 306 East Parr Road, Berne, IN 46711	39,200	Quarterly
Women's Sports and Fitness 809 S. Orlando Avenue Suite H, Winter Park, FL 32789	300,708	Monthly
World Tennis 3 Park Avenue New York, NY 10016	383,059	Monthly

Woodsman of the World Magazine 1700 Farnam Street Omaha, NE 68102	466,625	Monthly
Worldradio 2120 28th Street Sacramento, CA 95818	25,833	Monthly
Yachting 1515 Broadway New York, NY 10036	136,028	Monthly
Yoga Journal 2054 University Avenue Berkley, CA 94704	44,819	Monthly
Yankee Yankee Publishing, Inc. 4850 Gaidrew Road, Alpharetta, GA 30201	2,900,000	Monthly

Advertising in college papers

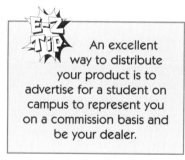

An excellent way to distribute your product is to advertise for a student on campus to represent you on a commission basis and be your dealer.

Colleges bulletins and newspapers have tremendous circulations. Their price per run on advertising is very inexpensive for the number of prospects reached. Believe it or not, multi-millions of dollars are spent by students each semester.

If you have a new idea or product, run a test ad in one or more of the publications and see if you get results. Usually a less expensive 1" ad will let you know whether your product or service is going to pull or not. If your test ad proves successful, then you may want to go to a larger ad or even a display-type ad and increase your coverage to include more bulletins and newspapers.

Usually there are several students who would love to have the opportunity to make some extra money. A good way to find the right person is by resume qualifications or actually calling them on the phone and talking it over with them. Finding the key person could result in many easy dollars in your pocket.

In the past, some of the biggest sellers on campus have been radio and stereo equipment, music tapes, car repair manuals, study aids, self-improvement booklets and tapes, school fads of various natures, and any kind of special or different steins for drinking beer. Any new idea or product you may be able to come up with could be very advantageous to you in the form of increased sales.

> *note* When ordering advertising, it is best to specify that your ad appear in the Monday-Wednesday editions.

Advertising in college bulletins and newspapers gains more results during the first three days of the week. Thursday is okay, but Friday is definitely out; minds seem to drift toward plans for the weekend, leaving little interest for purchasing.

Write to the enclosed list of publications. Ask for their rates and circulation. All of them will respond to your needs and many will call you and discuss whatever plans you have for advertising. They will work with you to try to see that you get the most response from any type ad you may run.

50 leading college buying powers

	Circulation
University of Oregon, *Daily Emerald*	
P.O. Box 3159, Eugene, OR 97403	10,500 daily
University of Arkansas, *Arkansas Traveler*	
Hill Hall 304, Fayetteville, AR 72701	8,000 bi-weekly
University of Mississippi, *Daily*	
Mississippi University, MS 38677	10,000 daily
University of Washington, *The Daily*	
144 Communications DS-20, Seattle, WA 98195	18,000 daily
University of Texas at Arlington, Student Publications	
P.O. Box 19038, Arlington, TX 76019-0038	18,000 daily
University of Virginia, *The Cavalier Daily*	
Newcomb Hall, Charlottesville, VA 22901	13,000 daily
Illinois State University, *Vidette*	
Normal, IL 61761	22,000 daily
Ball State University, Student Publications	14,000 daily
Muncie, IN 47306	
Florida State University, Student Publications	
P.O. Box U-7001, Tallahassee, FL 32306	46,000 daily
Jackson State University, Student Publications	
Jackson, MS 39217	Unknown

Indiana State University, *The Indiana Statesman*
Tirey Memorial Union
Annex, ISU Terre Haute, IN 47809   14,000 daily

West Texas State University, College of Arts and Science
Student Publications, Canyon, TX 79016   Unknown

Texas Southern University, Student Publications
3100 Cleburne Avenue, Houston, TX 77004   15,000 weekly

Spelman College, *Spelman Spotlight*
P.O. Box 40, Atlanta, GA 30314   Unknown

Wright State University, *The Daily Guardian*
Dayton, OH. 45435   4,000 daily

University of South Florida, *Oracle Let*
Arts and Letters Bldg., Tampa, FL 33620   25,000 daily

Ohio State University, *The Lantern*
281 Journalism Bldg., 242 W. 18th St.
Columbus, OH 43210-1107   31,000 daily

Montana State University, *Exponent Strand*
Union Bldg., Bozeman, MT 59715   8,000 bi-weekly

Texas Tech. University, Student Publications
P.O. Box 4080 Lubbock, TX 79409   17,000 daily

University of Florida, *The Alligator*
P.O. Box 14257, Gainesville, FL 32604   43,000 daily

Iowa University, Student Publications
111 Communications Center, Iowa City, IA 52242   20,000 daily

Bowling Green State University, *The BG News*
106 University Hall, Bowling Green, OH 43403   11,000 daily

Morgan State University, *Spokesman*
Cold Spring Ln. & Hillen Rd., Baltimore, MD 21239   4,000 bi-weekly

East Texas State University, *The East Texan*
Box D - ET Station, Commerce, TX 75428   7,000 bi-weekly

San Francisco State University, Dept. of Journalism
1600 Holloway Ave., San Francisco, CA 94132   10,000 weekly

Auburn University, *The Auburn Plainsman*
1st Floor, Foy Union Bldg,. Auburn, AL 36849   18,500 weekly

Winona State University, *Winonian*
Winona, MN 55987   Unknown

Washington University, *Student Life*
St. Louis, MO 63130   8,300 weekly

University of Tulsa, *Collegian*
600 So. College, Tulsa, OK 74104   4,000 weekly

University of Maryland, *Diamondback*
College Park, MD 20742   21,000 daily

University of Kentucky, *The Kentucky Kernel*
210 Journalism Bldg., Lexington, KY 40506   18,000 daily

Boston College, *The Heights*
Chestnut Hill, MA 02167   9,500 weekly

Seton Hall University, *The Setonian*
S. Orange, NJ 07079   10,500 Weekly

Pace University, *Pace*
Plaza New York, NY 10038   Unknown

University of New Mexico, Student Publications
P.O. Box 20, Albuquerque, NM 87131   30,000 weekly

University of Wisconsin, *Union*
Box 88 P.O. Box 413, Milwaukee, WI 53201   Unknown

University of Tennessee, Student Publications
5 Communications Bldg., Knoxville, TN 37996-0314   15,000 daily

Cal State University, Long Beach SS/PA-010
1250 Bellflower Blvd., Long Beach, CA 90840   20,000 daily

Northeastern University. *N.O. News*
360 Huntington Ave., Boston, MA 02115   21,000 weekly

University of Wisconsin, Stout *The Stoutonia*
Menomonie, WI 54751   7,000 weekly

Texas Christian University, *The Daily Skiff*
P.O. Box 32929   5,500 monthly

University of Wisconsin, Student Publications
La Crosse, WI 54601   5,000 weekly

Washington State University, *The Daily Evergreen*
P.O. Box 2008 C.S., Pullman, WA 99164   20,000 daily

San Jose State University, *Spartan Daily*
San Jose, CA 95192   15,000 daily

Portland State University, *Vaanguard*
P.O. Box 751, Portland, OR 97207   17,000 bi-weekly

Valdosta State College, *The Spectator*
VSC Box 194, Valdosta, GA 31698   Unknown

Kent State University, *Daily Kent*
Stater, Kent, OH 44242   Unknown

Georgia State University, *Signal*
Box 695, University Plaza, Atlanta, GA 30303   10,000 weekly

Arizona State University, State Press
15 Matthews Center, Tempe, AZ 85287   40,000 daily

Marketing and selling your product

5

Chapter 5

Marketing and selling your product

What you'll find in this chapter:

- ⟹ Where to find free advertising
- ⟹ The power of the free offer
- ⟹ 18 little-known tips
- ⟹ Low cost and no cost distribution
- ⟹ The power of mail order catalogs

Opportunities to get free advertising for your product or services are limited only by your own imagination and energies. There are so many proven ways of promoting your objectives without cost that it boggles the mind.

One way is to write an article relative to your particular expertise and submit it to all the publications and media dealing in related information. Establish yourself as an expert in your field, and "tag-along" everything you write with a quick note listing your address for a catalog, dealership opportunity, or more information.

Another really good way is by becoming a guest on as many radio and television talk shows or interview type programs as possible. Actually, this is much easier than most people realize. Write a letter to the producer of these

> **E-Z TIP**
> Become your own publicity and sales promotions writer. Get the word out!

programs, then follow-up with an in-person visit or telephone call. Your initial contact should emphasize that your product or service would be of interest to the listeners or viewers of the program, perhaps even saving them time and money.

Another way of getting free or very inexpensive exposure includes the posting of advertising circulars on all free bulletin boards in your area, especially the coin-operated laundries, grocery stores, and beauty and barber shops. Don't discount the idea of handing out circulars to all the shoppers in busy shopping centers and malls, especially on weekends. Some of the more routine methods include printing promotional ads about your product or service. Print them on the front or back of your envelopes when you print the envelopes with your return address.

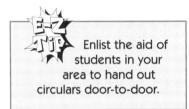
Enlist the aid of students in your area to hand out circulars door-to-door.

Be sure to check all the publications that carry the kind of advertising you need. Many new mail order publications, just getting started, offer unusually low rates to first-time advertisers. Free-of-charge insertion when you pay for an order to run three issues or more, or special seasonal ad space at greatly reduced rates are offered as well. And there are a number of publications that will give you *Per Inquiry (PI)* space-arrangement. In this case, when orders come in to the publication, they take a commission from each order, and then forward the orders to you for fulfillment.

Many publications will give you a contract for *"remnant"* space. Under this arrangement you send them your ad, and they hold it until they have unsold space. The price is always one third or less the regular price for the space. Along these lines, be sure to check the suburban neighborhood newspapers.

If you send or publish any kind of catalog or ad sheet, get in touch with all the other publishers and inquire about the possibilities of exchange advertising. They run your ad in their publication in exchange for you running a comparably sized ad for them in yours.

Simply run an ad offering a "free report" of interest to most people—a simple one page report with a "tag-line" inviting the readers to send money for more information. Include a full page advertisement for your book or other product on the reverse side. Ask for a self-addressed stamped envelope and, depending on the appeal for your report and circulation of the publication in which your ad appears, you could easily be inundated with responses!

> **note** There's nothing in the world that beats the low cost and tremendous exposure you get when you advertise a "free offer."

The trick here, of course, is to convert all these responses, or a large percentage of them, into sales. This is accomplished by the *"Tag Line,"* the full page ad on the back of the report, and other offers you include—all of which invite the reader to send for more information. Remember, it's just a matter of unleashing your imagination. Do that, and you have a powerful force working to help you reach your goals.

18 methods for obtaining free advertising

1) **Advertising specials:** If a magazine offers a "two for one" deal, or a "pay for 3 and get a fourth ad free," take advantage of it; it's free advertising!

2) **Free listings:** Some publications offer to list your name and address free, if you have something that you offer "free for the asking" to their readers. This can be a "free sample," a free list of customers; or whatever. Tell publishers what you have to offer.

3) **Print a booklet offering tips:** List tips and on the inside pages, or in the back, place some of your own free ads.

4) **The piggy-back method:** Every time you get ready to mail a letter or fill an order, place other ads in the envelope; it costs you no more and it's like getting a free ad!

5) **Free give-aways:** These can be pens, rulers, key chains, etc., each with YOUR ad message and address on each one. Give them away and your free ad rides along!

6) **Your own advertiser/newsletter:** Issue it regularly; sell ad space in it and subscriptions to it. They pay for the printing and postage, and YOUR ad is in it, too—at no cost to you.

7) **Trade products/services for ad space:** If you have something which a publisher needs, trade what they want, for ad space.

8) **Provide commission ads to dealers:** Your dealers place YOUR ads over THEIR name. Free ads for your products.

9) **Columns; releases, etc.:** Publishers will often print these free, if it's NEWS, or interesting to their readers. Send notices to editors and get free ads in exchange.

10) **Share costs with others:** Get together with other dealers and mailers. Split costs and quantities with others. Your ads go FREE to HIS customers, and HIS go free to yours.

11) **Offer your commission ads to publishers:** Publishers insert them as "mailer/distributor" commission ads. They cost you nothing and can get you lots of orders.

12) **Your product as a BONUS item on another's flyer:** This can increase the other person's orders, and YOUR product gets advertised on HIS flyers, etc.

13) **Place PIM-50 phrases in your ads:** This says to a publisher, "Insert my ad in your publication and I'll help distribute 50 (or

more) copies for you." It's another kind of "trade deal" with publishers.

14) **Give a talk or seminar:** Contact local clubs, and organizations. They always seek outside speakers. After you talk about your business or your product, hand out flyers, etc. It's like getting free advertising.

15) **Ads on bulletin boards:** Put up flyers on grocery, laundry bulletin boards.

16) **Make a rubber stamp of your ad:** Stamp it everywhere you can. Stamp it on envelopes, flyers, etc.

17) **Be listed as a source in back of books:** Often writers will want to list references and sources in their books. Get the word out to authors! Look for ads offering free ads.

18) **Discount to "a friend":** Tell your customers you will give discounts to anyone they send your way. It's word-of-mouth advertising; the best you can get and it's free.

Free advertising is any message that goes out to prospective buyers without cost to you. There are lots of ways to get others to spread the word about what you offer. Try these methods, and you'll get lots of free ads, which means more responses and more orders!

The cheapest way to distribute 8-1/2 X 11″ circulars

DEFINITION

Co-op mailing (short for *co-operative*) means two or more businesses share in the cost and distribution of a direct mail campaign—when you and another non-competing business split the cost of printing, assembling and mailing an advertising flyer to a shared (same) marketbase.

Co-op dealing is very beneficial (and usually safe) for everyone involved. One example of co-op dealing in mail order is to send your 8-1/2x11" camera-ready circular to a co-op printer and have them print your ad on one side, their ad on the back side and ship them back to you for a low cost of around $10 per 1,000. You get your printing almost free and the other dealer gets his or her flyers mailed on the back of yours, free.

But what do you do with them when they are mailed back to you? If you're new to mail order, it's doubtful you have a mailing list to distribute them. Plus, postage costs alone would run you about $330 first-class. At this rate, it would have been cheaper to send the camera-ready to a tabloid or adsheet publisher rather than use a co-op. But don't despair.

If this particular mailer sells a mailing list, have them do a 1,000 or 5,000 "test" mailing for you to test their names. You should get a few responses from a mailing of this size, but it all depends on what you are offering and the price you are offering it for. It's very difficult to sell any item for more than $50 on an 8-1/2x11" circular. For items costing more than $50, you need to use the two-step approach. In other words, use the 8-1/2x11" circular to generate inquiries and follow-up with the complete sales materials that constitute the higher price the customer may decide to pay.

Another idea is that you could contact a dealer with products and services not conflicting with your own and ask them to co-op mail for you. In this deal, you would pay for the 2-sided printing (with the mailer's ad on back of yours) and he/she would mail them for you free of charge. It works!

Another way to co-op deal in mail order is by co-op advertising. You place your ad the first time through a dealer and all future ads are 50% less.

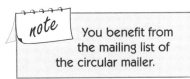

You benefit from the mailing list of the circular mailer.

Then you have the option of mailing pre-printed copies with your name in the publisher's block as an authorized dealer. When other people order advertising, they will send their orders to you. You keep 50% of the money and send the rest (along with the order) back to the publisher. This way, you can have your 8-1/2x11 circulars printed and mailed in a publication at a 50% savings.

> **note** Any beginner can handle mailing 50 circulars per week to a mailing list or to his own customers.

If you market the direct mail method, it's a good idea to send a good circular you plan to keep around for awhile to a mail order printer and have 1,000 printed on one side. Then, you can use the back of 100 or so for testing purposes of other circulars. Head down to the copy shop and run the circulars through the copier by printing on the back side. Only run 100 or less and send them to the best names you can find. If they pull orders, you may have a winner and can have 1,000 printed.

How to get 6,000 circulars printed and mailed free

Here is the plan that will enable you to get your circulars printed and mailed free, plus reduce the cost of your own mailing to zero.

> ⚠ **CAUTION** Nothing is more annoying than being stuck with 1,000 circulars with something you want to mail on one side and something outdated on the back.

Locate an offset printer in your area (or by mail order in one of the many mail order publications), who will print both sides of a 8-1/2 x 11 sheet for $25.00 per 1,000. Then run the following ad over your name in various mail order publications:

"Co-op printing (our ad on back side) 1,000 2-1/2 x 5-1/2, only $5.00. Send camera-ready copy to: (your name and address)."

"Circulars printed (our ad on back side). 1,000 3 x 6, only $5.00. Send camera-ready copy to: (your name and address)."

 On an 8-1/2 x 11 sheet of paper, you can get six 3 x 6 circulars which were received from responses to your ad, plus six 3 x 6's on the other side, free.

Have the printer cut them into six 3 x 6's, 1,000 each. Send 1,000 to each of your customers. You get 6,000 of your side printed free and mailed by your customers free.

Six responses to your ad will give you $30.00—$25.00 for printing and cutting and $5.00 for mailing circulars to your customers. When printing and postage costs rise, adjust your price accordingly. Maintain competitive prices.

There is another way to get your circulars mailed free. As soon as you can afford it, become a supplier of commission circulars. The easiest way to do this is to take "all profit" offers and have circulars printed on two sides. On one side, have your own name and address printed. On the other side, leave a space for a rubber stamp imprint.

 Offer these circulars to circular mailers on a commission basis. They keep a commission from 50% to 100% on the one side and you make your profit on the other. Use the same method for any offers that you develop for yourself.

You can reach these mailers by advertising in or subscribing to several mail order trade magazines and ad sheets. Another way to locate mailers for your literature is to notice the ads by mailers. At the bottom of their ads they usually state "commission circulars mailed free," which means they get one side and you get the other.

If you really want to get rolling using this method, take two "all profit" offers, one on each side, and give the mailer 100% on one side. You still make your profit on the other offer.

If you are interested in obtaining additional commission circulars for yourself, include "commission circulars mailed free" in your own ads.

 Still another way to get your literature mailed free is to include in all your advertising, at the end of the copy, this little note: "stamp appreciated." It only costs you two words, but it could save you a great deal in postage. If you are advertising in trade publications or adsheets use *"S.A.S.E."* which means *self addressed stamped envelope.* The savings of envelopes, addressing labor and postage can add up fast. Many small dealers use this method exclusively, even in large circulation magazines. They have been using it for years and it still works!

> *note* Check the mail order publications to see what others are charging for similar programs.

Sources of free commission circulars

This list was current at time of publication. However, suppliers sometimes change their policy. Most offer free circulars; you pay only the postage costs. Some suppliers are listed below:

A & M Sales Co., 3241 Haynes Ave., Chicago, IL 60618

Cavazos Advertising, 1952 S. King Rd., San Jose, CA 95122

Ace Products, Box 333, Shreveport, LA 71103

Atlanta Press, 1600 Hawthorne Dr., Chesapeake, VA 23325

Progressive Publications, Box 3770, Clear Lake Highlands, CA 95422

A & H Sales Co., Box 579, Cambridge, MD 21613

Astro Sales Co., Box 8901, Houston, TX 77009

Badburd Sales Co., 2559 Josephine St., Lynwood, CA 90262

Burco Sales Co., 39 Wyoming Ave., Ardmore, PA 19003

Barbies Shop, 347 Malden, Newport News, VA 22202

Chicago Mail Mart, 8408 Buffalo Ave, Chicago, IL 60617

Lew Card, Box 392, Vrea, CA 92621

Jack Clamp, Box 144, Hastings-on-Hudson, NY 10706

Cooleys Enterprises, Box 161, Signal Mtn., TN 37337

Danzig Enterprises, Box 142, Kensington Sta., Brooklyn, NY 11218

Dawde Enterprises, 9254 Manning Ave., Stillwater, MN 55082

Gradco Publications, Box 23436, Milwaukee, WI 53223

Ray Holder, Box 91, O'Keen, AR 72449

Midwest Mail Sales, Box 44RS, Shawano, WI 54166

Martels, Box 607, Median, ND 58134

Royal Sales Co., Box 17515, El Paso, TX 79914

Sandcos Publications, Box 3414, 9th St., Ceres, CA 95307

Success Publishers, Box 68, Webb City, MO 64870

Where to call for free printing, advertising and advice!

There are plenty of opportunities out there for you to get written materials free of charge, free advertising space, and free business advice.

 For free advertising space, many publications will write an article about you or your product if you purchase advertising space with them. One way publications sell advertising space is to agree that if the advertiser purchases the ad, he will also receive a certain amount of free editorial space. This free editorial space essentially doubles the amount of space you get for a given amount of money. This editorial space is devoted to an article about the company or individual or product, and it has the added benefit of seeming to be the work of an outside source. The editorial may be written by the publication staff, or the advertiser may provide the copy.

Sending press releases may lead to free space. The editor may even follow up with a phone call for more details. The result can be anything from a paragraph to a feature article. All this comes for the price of mailing the release. Keep in mind that you want to target the publication that writes about the kinds of things you are doing.

Many telephone call-in shows will take calls from entrepreneurs with interesting products or stories. You can get a media directory of stations around the country at your local library that you can contact to work out possibilities for free air time.

Marketing your own products and ideas

One of the main problems within the "inner circle" of the mail order business is that everyone is selling everyone else's products. Pages crammed full with commission dealerships is turning a good thing out of hand.

A well-written press release on an interesting subject will attract the editor's interest.

Newcomers to the industry should realize they need to develop their own products and services. Commission dealerships are fine to complement your business if the product is relative to your main product, but everyone should strive for developing their OWN product too. No one will ever get rich dealing in just commission dealerships.

How do you develop your own specialized product or service? It may take a few months to get your "feet wet" in mail order to determine your particular "niche." There has to be more to your business than making money!

What are your hobbies and interests? What would you like to do more than anything else? What would you do if you were not getting paid? For instance, I personally enjoy publishing newsletters. I get a surge of electricity when I am working on them. This is loving what you do.

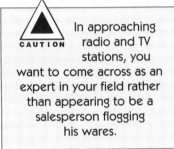

In approaching radio and TV stations, you want to come across as an expert in your field rather than appearing to be a salesperson flogging his wares.

On the other hand, perhaps you would rather write, edit, paste-up or seal envelopes. I remember "Dorothy" once explaining to me the "high" she used to get when doing a mass mailing. She loved peeling off labels, sticking them on envelopes and folding the materials to insert. She felt that every envelope she stuffed would generate a big customer order. This is enthusiasm!

Therefore, Dorothy could have developed a specialized or confidential mailing service. Unlike a big mail where she would be mailing circulars in envelopes, she would mail for different programs and products. (Example: A circular selling books and reports would be marketed only to book buyers from lists Dorothy would purchase and use for these types of mailings. She also would be careful not to put any conflicting information in this special mailing she was preparing for specific customers.)

A good friend of mine, Helen loved to prepare big mails so she created the "Design-Your-Own-Big-Mail-Package." Customers were presented with a list of the circulars Helen had on hand and they checked off the ones that interested them. This is one example of how an old concept can be turned into something new with a twist that makes it YOUR OWN product.

There are several ideas that other mail order folks have used to create their own product. You can use the same concept locally. If you sell vitamins, for instance, you could sell them in individual packets and label them for each day of the week. Use the vitamins from the company you are working with, but the individual packets and labels would be your own product. You can also charge more for this personal touch.

> *note* You should already know the talents you possess and what your own capabilities are.

You are unique! You are an individual who has special talents and interests. Mail order is a wonderful business, filled with some of the best people in the world. But it's up to every one of us to keep it that way.

Get your product listed and sold through mail order catalogs

An average mailing by a small, one person mail order company is generally about a thousand pieces, and many such operators rarely mail more than a hundred pieces per week. If you know your conversion statistics, you know that the order return on mailings is about 1% to 2% when using a rented list of names, up to 5% or more when mailing to your own customer list.

> *note* Keep in mind that these are catalog merchandisers. They are not manufacturers or publishers. They are mailers!

Using those figures, the response rate would be about 2 orders from a mailing of 100 when using a cold list, and about 5 to 10 orders when mailing to your own customer list for each 100 pieces mailed.

Contrast this with a major catalog mailing house such as Miles Kimball, Hanover House, Lillian Vernon, Johnson-Smith or L.L. Bean, each of which might consider a mailing of millions of pieces every few months.

What are they looking for?

Catalog houses are highly selective in the products they choose for inclusion in their catalogs. To even be considered, your product must pass some rigid tests:

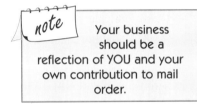
Your business should be a reflection of YOU and your own contribution to mail order.

- Since some catalog companies specialize in a certain type of merchandise, they will choose only what they think their customers will buy.

- Virtually all catalog companies will want to test-market a product (possibly only a hundred or so) before making a complete catalog mailing. If the test shows promise, they will purchase a large quantity (1,000 to 5,000 or more) for their roll-out mailings . . . and continue to purchase such quantities as long as the product continues to sell.

- Catalog mailers want to deal as close to the original source as possible, such as with the inventor, patent owner, copyright holder, manufacturer or publisher. The reason for this is simply

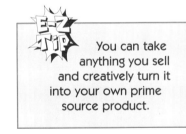
You can take anything you sell and creatively turn it into your own prime source product.

that they can offer them the largest discount on quantity purchases. If you are merely one of many dealers who had to purchase the product from a wholesaler who purchased from a distributor, who purchased the product from the manufacturer, you would not be in a position to offer the lowest price to the catalog company.

- The item in question should be new and unique, not something that's been around for years. Naturally, it should be a good mail order item.

How you can qualify

First and foremost, you must look and act the part of an established, professionally operated business. This means you must have printed stationery with a company name that coincides with the products you are offering, and all correspondence must be typewritten.

If that seems elementary, you would be surprised to see how many companies receive scribbled handwritten notes on ruled paper with wording such as "I would like you to include my product in your catalog." Sorry, it just doesn't work like that.

Even if you are not the actual inventor or manufacturer of the product you are selling, you can qualify to have it included in a large mailers' catalog where everyone can profit from it. Imports are very popular catalog sellers, for instance, so if you locate a new item from overseas, you can arrange to become the U.S. distributor. Yes, it means a sizable investment for stocking inventory, but if you have faith in what you plan to sell, it should be worth investing in.

Before offering it to any catalog mailer, however, it would be in your best interest to test-market the item yourself. You'll want to be sure this is something that will sell, so everybody is happy with the deal. Perhaps, even more importantly, it will bond your relationship with the catalog companies and they will be eager to do business with you the next time you come up with a new product.

Pricing your product

This is crucial. A price that's too high means it will not be accepted; priced too low and you will not make a profit . . . no matter how many are sold.

Keep in mind that some catalog mailers specialize in low priced ($10 or less) items, while others have geared their sales to the higher bracket of $50 or more. When making a list of catalog houses to approach, check their catalogs for prices of their current merchandise.

There are three basic levels of retail prices:

1) the pre-established price by owner or manufacturer

2) actual dollar value based on production costs

3) perceived value by prospective buyers

note

If you are not the primary source for your product, the manufacturer may have already set the retail price along with distributor and wholesale discounts, so you will have to work those figures in any deals made with catalog companies.

Assuming you have pricing control (granted by the original source, or you are the originator), you can set the retail price according to the production costs which can be a 5-to-1 or 10-1 ratio. If the item costs $1 to make, you can set a retail price of $5 to $10 on it, depending on what you think it is worth to the consumer.

Simplify your price structure to companies

The most common price structures are usually set in various quantities like a dozen or gross or 100, 500, 1,000, etc. Don't use these price structures when trying to interest catalog companies in your product.

For example: If your usual prices are: 100 @ $4.50; 500 @ $3.75; 1,000 @ $2.75 and 5,000 @ $1.95 give them your 5,000 quantity price no matter how many they order for their original test. Even if they only want 100 for testing, give them your $1.95 price . . . but be sure to tell them this is your lowest price for regular 5,000 quantity purchases, so they know they're getting the good deal.

Time to create your promotional package

Company buyers are busy people, so you'll want to make your presentation quickly, clearly, and distinctly, eliminating all fluff and extraneous material or wording that might tend to bog things down.

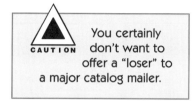 You certainly don't want to offer a "loser" to a major catalog mailer.

Here's what you'll need:

- descriptive folder or flyer about the product (information sheet)

- glossy photo of the product

- possible advertising copy (although they will probably re-write it)

- terms of your sale, including freight charges

- brief cover letter

- (Optional) sample of your product IF it is small, lightweight, inexpensive, and if you think it will impress the company

Send this mailing package via First Class Mail!

How many of these promotional packages should you mail? Only you can answer that question, but here's a tip: Don't expect only 10 or 12 to produce much response for your product. It might require 50 to 100 or even 500 such mailings before you begin to see worthwhile results. Of course, a lot depends on the product itself and whether it is for the general public or restricted to a more selective audience.

If the catalog caters only to men and your product will be used primarily by women, why waste time and money? The same would apply to a low-priced item, offered to a catalog house whose clientele happened to be sophisticated, wealthy people accustomed to buying merchandise in the hundreds of dollars. Match your product with the catalog company's line as closely as possible.

Handling the business

If your product is a good one, and, if you made a good impression in your promotional materials, sooner or later you will get an order for a trial quantity.

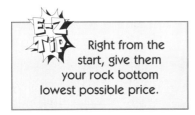

Right from the start, give them your rock bottom lowest possible price.

Fill the order promptly. Use sturdy boxes and have your own shipping label (printed with your company name and address) on each carton, typing the catalog company's name and address with the customer's shipping number above the name.

Selling on credit

Unlike the conventional mail order business, selling to catalog houses is not a cash-with-order type of operation. It's conducted on credit, so you'll need invoices to send to your customer after shipment has been made. There are a few variations of credit terms, but the best for you will be "Payment due EOM or 2% discount within 10 days," EOM means end of the month following the date of shipment. Use your best judgment whether you will ship prepaid or bill your customer for the shipping charges.

Here's a final tip

Check magazines that are read by the type of people who will use your product and look for departments such as "New Products." Many magazines carry such a department under different titles.

Send a publicity package to the editors which will include the glossy photo of your product, news release that tells who will be interested in the product and why, and a brief cover letter.

Whenever possible, try to determine what type of merchandise each catalog house offers before sending them your offer.

If you get a few magazines to accept your offer, they will give you a mention in their New Products department. This will, in turn, bring you orders, depending on the circulation of the magazines and how much demand there might be for your product.

More importantly, it can link you up with some catalog houses. They often scan magazines looking for new products to be featured in their catalogs. Thus, instead of you contacting them . . . they will contact you.

The end result is that it can bring you many retail orders as well as attract a few catalog house buyers who will ultimately sell your product in their catalogs. If each catalog house mails 10 million catalogs a year, and your product is featured inside, be prepared for the number of products that can be sold this way. Better stock up now!

How mail-order works for you

6

Chapter 6

How mail-order works for you

The following are three examples of successful advertisements used to sell the *"ABC's of RED HOT Name Lists."* Use these as models for your own creative ads. Pay careful attention to the construction of each ad as you substitute your own words.

Full page circular, example 1

BRAND NEW ALL-PROFIT PROGRAM FOR YOU.
ABC'S of RED-HOT Name Lists.
THE NEW MANUAL YOU CAN PRINT & SELL. ALL MAILERS NEED
THIS TO SUCCEED!

INSIDE SECRETS REVEALED NOW! For the first time, you'll be shown exactly how the professionals make their money in this fascinating business. You'll be able to use all these special secrets and tricks-of-the-trade for your benefit.

You'll also learn all the angles used by mailing lists experts to make their customers order repeatedly. And, you'll have the simple, but oh-so-powerful, techniques used to subtly command an order from your prospect.

PARTIAL LIST OF TOPICS COVERED: Name lists and their use; What buyers look for when selecting a list; How to get started; How and where to get names; How much to pay; How the "big boys" get their names; How to use a drop-ship supplier to build your business; How to start with little money; What you should know about advertising; How to computerize your list; How to protect your names; How to correctly run your business; How to sell your lists; How to obtain and keep customers; How to insure winning ads; How to buy lists from other dealers; Name lists; A profit center for you; How to protect your lists; Plus much, much more; All the facts and figures you'll need to get started immediately!

WHY THE MAILING LIST BUSINESS IS SO PROFITABLE! Unlimited market. No high start up costs. No need for employees. Product cost is low. High profit margin. Large amount of re-orders. Sales are not seasonal. Easy to start and operate. Can be run on a part-time or full-time basis. No special skills or education required. Yields excellent profits. A business that you and your family can be proud of.

DON'T WASTE VALUABLE TIME! Don't flounder around for years trying to find the right methods and systems. Learn all the facts, now, right at the start. Save time and money by using both wisely and correctly.

All instructions are written in clear, precise, easy-to-understand, and put into practice language. You'll be able to proceed at your own pace. Nothing is left dangling. You'll get practical information—no fancy theories—no amateur suggestions—strictly valuable professional pointers.

If you have a list to sell, here's your chance. If you don't have a list, this will show you exactly, in a step-by-step manner, how to acquire all the names you'll need.

Start on a shoestring if you wish. Build a business that will pay you an income for the rest of your life. Remember, a mailing list business can be operated from any location, any state, any city or rural area.

GET STARTED NOW!—FOR ONLY $10. INCLUDES FULL REPRODUCTION RIGHTS to this complete program PLUS this powerful sales circular!

BIG MONEY NEWS: When you order the "RED-HOT" program for just $10, you also receive full reprint rights! This means you can print the entire program—as well as this dynamic circular—and earn over $9.50 profit on every sale! A prize-winner that can spell "P-R-O-F-I-T-S" for YOU!

Bonus: Act today and we will include 8 sample circulars and ads, which you can use to sell your new mailing lists!

(order coupon)

_____O.K. Enclosed is $10. Please rush the complete "RED-HOT" program. I understand I have full reprint rights to the entire program, plus this big circular.

Full page circular, example 2

FRESH RESPONSIVE MAILING LISTS THAT DELIVER
OPPORTUNITY SEEKERS

CASH BUYERS All proven mail order buyers. Our names are excellent for any type of money-making offer including multi-level marketing.

People have spent $20 to $500 and more, on Mail Order MONEY-MAKING OPPORTUNITIES.

Show them how to make money or sell something that makes money and they will respond.

IF YOUR OFFER DOESN'T PULL TO THESE NAMES, IT JUST WON'T PULL!

OUR LISTS ARE DIFFERENT. We gather our own BUYERS, OPPORTUNITY SEEKERS . . . Accurate records are kept. Buyers NEVER receive duplicate names. Most important, WE make a LIMITED number of copies so the names are NEVER overworked.

We maintain and collect our own lists—NO brokers fees—No middlemen . . . We pass all these savings on to you at extremely LOW PRICES for such high quality names.

WE CONSIDER THE RENTING OF OUR MAILING LISTS TO BE A VITAL PART OF OUR BUSINESS. OUR PRICES ARE RIGHT. OUR SERVICE IS PROMPT AND ACCURATE, AND YOU CAN TEST AS FEW AS 100 NAMES.

GUARANTEED 100% DELIVERABLE: Return any undeliverable piece, front face of envelope within 45 days and we will replace with 10 fresh names for each one returned . . . (please note) Our names are rented for ONE TIME USE ONLY . . . They may not be copied, duplicated or resold under any circumstances. Names are on pressure sensitive "PEEL & STICK" labels. All sharp, clear and zip-coded.

If you are a mailer, you owe it to yourself to test these names. Once they work for your offer, you will have a whole new market for your product or service.

SEND US A TRIAL TEST ORDER TODAY, and you be the judge. We know of no better lists that you can get anywhere at any price. When you place your order for a trial test, we suggest you send a copy of your mailing piece(s) so as to avoid conflicting offers mailed to the same group of names.

Complete order form below, detach and enclose in the convenient return envelope.

(order form)

Personal checks warmly accepted—all orders filled same day received. (Orders shipped FIRST CLASS U.S. PRIORITY MAIL)

[*provide a price list, as follows:*] TEST TRIAL OFFER 100 names—$9; 200 names—$14; 500 names—$25, etc.

Full page circular, example 3

COMPUTERIZED LISTS OF MAIL ORDER BUYERS IN
DOZENS OF CATEGORIES

That's right! Thousands of firms and individual express their confidence in us each year by allowing us to satisfy their most discriminating mailing list needs.

CATEGORIES OF BUYERS:

201-Opportunity seekers/actual buyers
202-Novelty buyers
203-Mail order enthusiasts/buyers
204-Sales agents/buyers
205-Catalog buyers
206-Adult product buyers
207-Mail order jewelry buyers
208-Education buyers
209-Home working buyers
210-Religious product buyers
211-Membership buyers
212-Record and tape buyers
213-Music lovers
214-Antique buyers
215-Collectors
216-Executives
217-Diet program buyers
218-Automotive buff buyers
219-Vacation and travel buyers
220-Boating product buyers
221-Demonstration agent kit buyers
222-Indoor hobby buyers
223-Outdoor hobby buyers
224-Art buyers
225-Small business buyers
226-CB radio buyers

227-Charge account buyers   228-Club membership buyers

229-Contributors   230-Fund raising prospects

231-Gift buyers   232-Photography buyers

233-Electronic buyers   234-Franchise prospects

235-Sports enthusiasts   236-Book buyers

237-Gourmet food buyers   238-Gambling system buyers

239-Car stereo buyers

Special Categories Available Upon Request.

The key to your future success could very well be the right source for mailing lists, and our mailing lists are our specialty. This means we can zero in on the exact type of individual that is most likely to respond to your offer. This type of service is uncommon in the list business and we want to serve you!

(insert your order form)

Personal checks warmly accepted—all orders filled same day received. (Orders shipped FIRST CLASS U.S. PRIORITY MAIL)

What is a qualified name?

DEFINITION

Simply stated, there are basically three types of names used when a mailing list is compiled. First, there are *saturation names*. These are names in a given geographic area and usually consist of every household. Lists of this nature are often used by churches or political parties, but are never successful for mail order offers because the interests of the recipients are too varied.

Second, there are lists of people who have inquired about various products or services. *Inquiry mailing lists,* although far superior to saturation lists or phone book names in mail order offers, often do not produce the results that are necessary to obtain an adequate profit.

Third, there are *actual buyers* of products or services. These people have spent their hard-earned money before on mail order offers. It is therefore logical to assume that they will do so again. Thus, buyers lists are the best and most responsive.

Beware of cheap mailing lists

Sometimes you'll see mailing lists offered at extremely low prices. You'll get exactly what you paid for. In almost all cases, the names you get will be photocopied on to labels and not in zip order (you need a computer to do that). The print will be of poor quality and some names will be illegible. And most important, without a computer you cannot update a mailing list or delete the nixies. Consequently, you'll waste a lot of money on printing and postage for undeliverables.

Buying or renting?

Quality list sources rent names for one-time use. Each list may have a few "dummy" names on it. This is how list services protect lists from being duplicated and reused. This *"salting"* procedure not only keeps lists from being stolen, but it ensures the quality for customers.

What about those who respond?

When you buy a list, individuals who order from remain your customers and you can remail to those names as often as you please. Eventually, you have enough names to build your own mailing list. This list will be your best because these people are already acquainted with you, your company, and your product.

Bulletin board advertising service

7

Chapter 7

Bulletin board advertising service

Bulletin boards serve to enhance the community relations image of a business, and the space required to locate a bulletin board can be written off as a tax deduction when listed as an advertising or public relations expense.

note Bulletin boards actually work as traffic builders for small business.

People use these "business provided" bulletin boards to advertise things they want to sell, home-based businesses, and whatever they want to trade for or buy. Then they come back every day to check them, or to see who else has posted an announcement. Each time they come into the business owner's store or shop, the business owner has another opportunity to sell them something.

Just about anybody can organize a route of bulletin boards; charge the advertisers a small monthly fee; keep them up-to-date and neat, (which will make the business owner happy) and make some really easy money in the whole process.

Sell store owners the idea of allowing you to install and maintain a bulletin board service for them.

The first step is to contact as many businesses in your area as possible. Grocery stores, drugstores, barber shops, beauty salons, service stations, quick print shops, rental shops, mobile home parks, shopping centers, apartment complexes that have foyers or recreation rooms, and the list goes on endlessly.

Emphasize the community service, the tax write-off, and the fact that you'll keep it neat. When ten or more agree to allow you to install a bulletin board, you're ready to start making your bulletin boards.

The best plan and, of course, the most economical, is to make your own. Cut a piece of corkboard 3 feet by 4 feet, mount a 3/4 by 1 1/2 inch frame around the edge, and cover this frame with a 3 foot by 4 foot piece of plastic. Mount the plastic with hinges at the top and hasp at the bottom. On the back of the corkboard, install a couple of hooks for hanging and you're ready to go.

Make a sign—you can even type it and use it as another bulletin board announcement, something like this:

City-wide bulletin board services

Your announcement or advertisement displayed here for only $5 per month! For more information, call _____(*your phone number*).

Put your sign or announcement on each of your bulletin boards, lock them up, and install them in all your locations. Ten signs with only 50 announcements per bulletin board should bring you an additional $500 per month.

When you put an announcement from the same person up on more than one board, charge them $5 per announcement on each bulletin board. And one other thing: The date the "run of display" ends should be marked on each announcement on each of your bulletin boards.

In all likelihood, you'll have people waiting for space on your bulletin boards. Keeping records should be very simple and easy. Start with a loose leaf notebook, blank paper and a couple of packages of 3 by 5 cards. In your notebook, write down the date, the amount of money received, the number of announcements on display, and the contract expiration date. On the 3 by 5 cards, write name, address, phone number and expiration date of each contract, and the location(s) of the bulletin boards(s) that particular announcement is on. Arrange the cards in chronological order according to expiration date, and file them in a storage box.

Take the feature editors out to lunch, make friends with them, and push for all the free publicity you can get.

Once you get rolling, you shouldn't have to service your bulletin boards more than once a week, and as more people see them, more businesses will want you to put one in their business location, and more people will want to display announcements. Simple, easy and a money-maker for you.

This kind of business is what the newspapers like to write about, and the TV stations like to carry as news about what the entrepreneurs in their areas are doing.

It demands little investment, not much of your time and no special training or education. But, as with any business venture, it takes ACTION on your part. You must get out there and set it up, and work at making it a success for YOU!

Free TV, movie and radio advertising

Chapter 8

Free TV, movie and radio advertising

What you'll find in this chapter:

- ➡ What P.I. advertising can do for you
- ➡ Putting the ad package together
- ➡ Using your products as props
- ➡ Creating the introduction
- ➡ Ways to follow-up

The greatest expense you are liable to incur in conducting a successful business is advertising. You have to advertise. Your business cannot grow and flourish unless you advertise. Regardless of where or how you advertise, it's going to cost you in some form or another.

Advertising is the "life-blood" of any profitable business.

Every successful business is built upon and continues to thrive primarily upon good advertising. The top companies in the world allocate millions of dollars annually to their advertising budget. Of course, when starting from a garage, basement or kitchen table, you can't quite match their advertising efforts—at least not in the beginning. But there is a way you can approximate their strategies without actually spending their kind of money. And that's through "P.I." advertising.

How to get free radio advertising

"P.I." stands for *per inquiry*. This kind of advertising is most generally associated with broadcasting—you pay only for the responses you receive **DEFINITION** from your advertising message. It's very popular and somewhat akin to bartering. It is used by many more advertisers than most people realize. The advantages of P.I. advertising are all in your favor because you pay only for the results the advertising produces.

To get in on this "free" advertising, start with a loose leaf notebook, and about 100 sheets of filler paper. Next, either visit your public library and start poring through the *Broadcasting & Cable Yearbook* for radio stations in the U.S., or the *Standard Rate and Data Services Directory* (SRDS) on Spot Radio. Both these publications will give you just about all the information you could ever want about licensed stations.

An easier way might be to call or visit one of your local radio stations, and ask to borrow their current copy of either of these volumes.

Once you have a copy of either of these publications, select the state or states you want to work first. It's generally best to begin in your own state and work outward. If you have a moneymaking manual, start first with those states reporting the most unemployment.

Use some old-fashioned common sense. Who are the people most likely to be interested in your offer, and where are the largest concentrations of these **CAUTION** people? You wouldn't attempt to sell windshield de-ice canisters in Florida, or suntan lotion in Minnesota during the winter months, would you?

At any rate, once you've decided your beginning target area, go through the radio listings for the cities and towns in that area, and jot down the names of general managers, the station call letters, and addresses. Be sure to list the telephone numbers as well.

On the first try, list only one radio station per city. Pick out the station people most interested in your product are likely to listen to. Determine this by the programming description contained within the date block about the station in the *Broadcasting Yearbook* or the *SRDS Directory*.

 The first contact should begin with an introduction and inquire if they would consider a P.I. advertising campaign. Tell the station manger you have a product you feel will sell very well in his market, and would like to test it before proceeding with a paid advertising program. You must quickly point

out that your product sells for, say $10, and that during this test, you would give the station 50% of the price for each response the station pulls for you. Explain that you handle everything: writing the commercials, | *note* Your contact letter should be positive in tone, straightforward and complete.

all accounting and bookkeeping, plus any necessary refunds or complaints. In other words, all they have to do is schedule your commercials in their log, and give it their "best shot." When the responses come in, the station counts them and forwards them to you for fulfillment. You make out a check, pay the station, and everybody is happy.

If you've contacted the station by phone, and they agree to look over your material, thank them and promise to mail a complete package immediately. Do just that! Write a short cover letter, place it on top of your "ready-to-go" P.I. advertising package, and mail it without delay. If you're turned down, just thank them, make a notation in your notebook by the station name, and go to your next call.

Contacting the station managers by phone is by far the quickest, least expensive and most productive method of "exploring" those stations willing to consider your P.I. proposal. In some cases though, it will be less expensive to make this initial contact by letter or postcard.

In that case, simply address your card or letter to the person you are trying to contact. Present all the details in logical order on one page, perfectly typed on letterhead paper, and sent in a letterhead envelope. (Rubber-stamped letterheads just won't get past a first glance.) Ideally, you should include a self-addressed and stamped postcard with spaces for positive or negative check marks in answer to your questions: Will you or won't you look over my material and consider a mutually profitable "Per Inquiry" advertising campaign on your station?

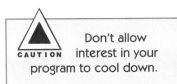

Don't allow interest in your program to cool down.

Once you have an agreement from your contact at the radio station that they will look over your materials and give serious consideration for a P.I. program, move quickly. Send your cover letter and package by First Class mail, or perhaps even special delivery.

At the same time as you organize your radio station notebook, you'll also want to organize your advertising package. Have it all put together and ready to mail just as soon as you receive a positive response.

You'll need a follow-up letter. Write one to fit all situations; have 250 copies printed and then, when you're ready to send out a package, all you have to do is fill in the business salutation and sign it. If you spoke of different arrangements or a specific matter was discussed in your initial contact, type a different letter incorporating comments or answers to the points discussed. This personal touch won't take long, and could pay big dividends!

You'll also need at least two 30-second commercials and two 60-second commercials. You should write these, and have 250 copies printed and organized as a part of your P.I. advertising package.

You should also have an *advertising contract* drawn up. It must detail everything about your program, how everything is to be handled, how and when payment to the radio station is to be made, plus special paragraphs relative to refunds, complaints, and liabilities. All this can be quickly drawn up and printed in lots of 250 or more on carbonless multi-part snap-out business forms.

Finally, include a self-addressed and stamped postcard the radio station can use to let you know that they are going to use your P.I. Advertising program, when they will start running your commercials on the air, how often, and during which time periods. Again, simply type out the wording in the form you want to use on these "reply postcards," and have copies printed for these mailings.

> **note** When turned down by the station, simply say thanks, and go to the next station on the list.

To review this program: Your first step is the initial contact after searching through the *SRDS* or *Broadcasting Yearbook*. Actual contact with the stations is by phone or mail. To those who want to know more about your proposal, immediately send a P.I. advertising package. Don't let the interest wane.

Your advertising package should contain the following:

- cover letter

- sample brochure and product literature

- 30-second and 60-second commercials

- P.I. advertising contract

- Self-addressed, stamped postcard for station acknowledgment and acceptance of your program

Before you ask why you need an acknowledgment postcard when you have already given them a contract, remember, everything about business changes from day-to-day. Conditions change, people get busy, and other things come up. The station manager may sign a contract for your advertising to begin the 1st of March. The contract is signed on the 1st of January, but when March 1st rolls around, he may have forgotten, been replaced, or even decided against running your program. A lot of paper seemingly "covering all the minute details" can be very impressive to many radio station managers, and convince them that your company is a good one with which to do business.

Let's say that right now you're impatient to get started with your own P.I. Advertising campaign. Before you "jump off the deep end," remember this: Radio station personnel are just as professional and dedicated as anyone else in business so be sure you have a product or service that lends itself well to selling via radio.

> **note**
> Anything can be sold, and sold easily, with any method you decide upon, providing you present it from the right angle.

"Hello out there! Who wants to buy a mailing list for 10 cents a thousand names?" wouldn't even be allowed on the air. However, if you have the addresses of the top 100 movie stars, and you put together an idea enabling people to write to them directly, you might have a winner, and sell a lot of "mailing lists of the stars."

The bottom line is riding on the content of your commercial—the benefits you suggest to the listener, and how easy it is for him to enjoy those benefits. For instance, if you have a new book on how to find jobs when there aren't any jobs, you want to talk to people who are searching for employment. You have to appeal to them in words that not only "perk up" their ears, but cause them to feel that whatever it is you're offering will solve their problems. It's the product, and the advertising message about that product, that are going to bring in those responses.

Radio station managers are sales people, and sales people the world over will be sold on your idea if you put your sales package together properly. When the responses come in your first offer, you have set yourself up for an entire series of successes. Success has a ripple effect, but you have to start with that first one.

Using your products as a prop in a movie or TV show

DEFINITION

Casual advertising is one of the most effective ways to present your product to the market. By placing them as props in movies or TV shows, your product is exposed to a wide audience base, and with some implied level of endorsement.

To be able to do this, it is customary, even essential, to hire a broker who specializes in placing products in movies and TV shows. For movies, brokers work out the details of placing your product in a film and guarantee that the product will be used in a very positive way. For TV shows, the most common areas are game shows where your product can be given away as a prize or mentioned as a prize sponsor. (Dramatic or comedy TV shows, including series and soaps, refuse to take "casuals" because of the conflict it may create with regular sponsors of the show.)

> *note* When Clark Kent spooned Cheerios into his mouth in the movie *Superman,* it was not because the director or the writers found it essential or entertaining. It was the result of a negotiation made between the film's producers and General Mills.

CAUTION

Movie casuals may cost around $25,000. Of course, the price varies, depending on the stars of the film, the length of time it will be held up on screen, and your products' identifiable role in the movie.

One way to locate a broker: visit the site of the Entertainment Resources & Marketing Association—http://www.erma.org

Infomercial marketing

Chapter 9

Infomercial marketing

Infomercials now serve as standard fare. In fact, references to those late-night infomercials on TV are no longer accurate, because infomercials now air and make money during daytime and midday hours as well, selling every conceivable product, from Ginsu knives to "Body by Jake."

What is an infomercial?

DEFINITION

The term *infomercial* refers to a very specific form of TV advertising. Let's break apart the pieces and identify the ingredients of an infomercial:

- **It is an ad!** First and foremost, an infomercial is simply another form of advertisement. It is a commercial message, and represents the viewpoints and serves the interest of the sponsor. It is a "paid program."

- **It is long form!** Unlike conventional 30 and 60 second TV ads, an infomercial runs at least a half hour. The reason: a half-hour is the smallest block of airtime a TV station will sell without interrupting its programming schedules. (NO program on TV is shorter than 30 minutes.)

- **It solicits a "direct" response!** An infomercial must solicit a response which is specific and quantifiable. The solicitation and the delivery of the response must be direct between the advertiser and the viewer.

The list of official sounding names, from "documercials" to "long-form advertising," or "paid programming," is endless and can be confusing. Some terms do not adequately define the scope of this new form of advertising.

> *note* For a month's rent, an infomercial can be aired on cable stations that reach 60 million homes nationwide.

For example, the term *long-form advertising* seems to be a favorite among media people. Unfortunately, the term describes only the time aspect, disregarding purpose and content. Of course, it does reflect the focus of those in TV circles, as opposed to the broader perspective of those in the marketing community. What will become of the term *long-form advertising* when paid advertising programs extend to an hour or longer? Will the term be upgraded to "longer-form advertising" and then "longest-form advertising?"

By contrast, the term *direct response advertising* is obviously of a marketing heritage. But like the former, the term is incomplete because it does not qualify the medium being used.

Finally, there are those who feel uncomfortable with the term infomercial because it sounds too gimmicky or colloquial. However, more and more companies are accepting and using the term *infomercial,* and because of that, the name will probably stand the test of time.

What are DRTV spots?

DEFINITION

The term *DRTV spot (Direct Response Television)* refers to standard length direct response advertisements that are aired within or between regularly scheduled programs.

Like infomercials, DRTV spots are designed to solicit a specific direct response from the TV viewers. Although standard length is usually one or two minutes, DRTV spots may run anywhere from ten seconds to three minutes.

> **note**
>
> Unlike infomercials, DRTV spots are not program-length ads.

Your product and the type of response you are trying to generate will dictate when DRTV spots may be more cost-effective than infomercials, and vice versa.

Direct response television is faster and more effective than conventional mail order in marketing products direct to the end users for several reasons:

- **It's audio visual.** Direct response television presents your sales message with both sound and pictures.

- **It's instantaneous.** You can monitor your sales results seconds after your message is delivered.

- **It's cost-effective.** Airing your infomercial may cost less than a conventional mail order campaign. Example: You can buy a half hour of airtime at WXYZ station and reach over 200,000 homes for around $300. With conventional mail marketing, $300 will only buy 909 first class stamps. Add to that the cost of mailing lists, production, and printing of your mailing piece.

The future of marketing is in the consumer's own living room, in the TV set, where a new, more convenient way of shopping is taking shape.

For the advertiser, the reasons for using infomercials and DRTV are obvious. Producing a half-hour infomercial is a lot cheaper than opening a new store in the mall.

If you're looking for a new frontier with growth potential, DRTV is an exciting new territory with no boundaries—a territory that has all the ingredients for success you'll ever need.

The birth of DRTV

A comparison of infomercials and DRTV spots with all types of TV advertising from 30 years ago reveals what made direct response TV advertising feasible. Three services made available during the last decade are what made direct response television possible. They are:

- **Toll free numbers:** The consumer is now able to respond or interact directly with the advertiser. The numbers are widely available, convenient, and most importantly, free to the consumer.

- **Proliferation of credit cards:** Over 100 million credit cards are in circulation in the U.S. This tool enables a huge number of consumers to make purchases over the telephone.

- **Overnight delivery:** To get consumers to respond to your sales offer right away, make sure you give them the satisfaction of having your product right away.

- **Merchant account:** Service bureaus that handle order taking for you will almost certainly require you to have your own merchant account. Without a merchant account, you will not be able to accept credit card payments. Needless to say, this will seriously affect your overall sales figures.

If you do not have your own merchant account to process credit card orders, it is essential that you use a service bureau or enter into a joint marketing venture with a company that is able to extend you this privilege.

Accepting checks over the phone

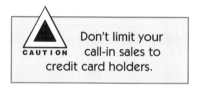

Don't limit your call-in sales to credit card holders.

By expanding the way TV viewers can pay for their purchases, you increase your probability of making a sale (with the introduction of checks-by-phone, your potential market is likely to grow by another 30%). Check verification makes your product available to millions of people who do not have a credit card, but do have a checking account. Here are some practical reasons why you should consider accepting check orders over the phone:

- **It commits the buyer:** The buyer doesn't have to write a check, write his name and address on a piece of paper, look for an envelope, get postage, and then mail the order. These steps can take anywhere from a few minutes to a few days. The longer it takes, the higher the odds your potential buyer will change his mind.

- **Instant gratification:** Your customer's order can be cleared and processed faster if he doesn't have to mail a check which your bank has to clear before the order is processed. With check verification, you get the money within 48 hours and your customer receives the product sooner.

- **Competitive rates:** If your ticket price is over $59, your unit cost to process a check order by phone will be almost the same as the commission the bank charges your merchant account. As this service become more readily available, and as merchant accounts become more difficult to acquire, accepting check orders over the telephone is a feature DRTV marketers can no longer ignore.

> *note*
>
> The best way to promote a continuity item is through a brochure or other sales literature inserted with the original order.

- **Continuity programs:** Develop a product or service that will fit into your back-end marketing program. Remember, the easiest person to sell is one who has already purchased from you. A continuity program will produce sales from customers who have just made a purchase through an infomercial.

Developing a successful continuity program will enhance your bottom line, particularly since your advertising message is usually delivered at no additional expense to you. Furthermore, your continuity item is being offered to satisfied customers, because your company made their TV buying pleasant and satisfying.

Seek related items

Continuity items should normally be related to the initial product. The consumer purchases your initial product to satisfy a specific need, so it stands to reason that auxiliary products catering to this same need stand a higher chance of success than totally unrelated products.

For example: If an exercise machine is your main product in the infomercial, a monthly vitamin subscription plan can be an ideal continuity program. It is related to the customer's original need (to be healthy and fit), and you can count on a profit margin because your advertising costs for the vitamin subscription are minimal.

Relationship marketing

Continuity may also be looked at as a means to establish a marketing relationship with your customers. Through profile response cards and other dynamic data, you can produce a catalog that features several products that cater to the needs and wants defined by your customer base.

As the cost of acquiring new customers increases, selling more to the same customers expands the potential for DRTV in almost any market.

To continue with the example above, you can offer your customer (who originally purchased exercise equipment via your infomercial) a wide variety of products and services in a catalog—duffel bags, running shorts, portable CD players, you name it.

Be your own competition

When a product becomes an infomercial success story, competitors try to duplicate your product and your marketing campaign. Such competitors are called knock-offs.

DEFINITION

In most cases, *knock-offs* are cheaper versions—in both quality and price. However, one of the most brilliant knock-off DRTV campaigns broke all the files:

- The company introduced a product of a higher quality and at a higher price than the original.

- Both products came from the same company, so the company was actually competing against itself.

- The same celebrity hosted the infomercials for both products.

165

The product was *Stair Climber Plus,* an upscale version of its predecessor, *Super Step.* Both infomercials featured Bruce Jenner, clearly showing the manufacturer's intent to present competition that did not exist— in the process preempting any legitimate competition. Neither infomercial mentioned the other product and, for a while, they were running at the same time.

What does this strategy achieve?

Producing your own knock-offs, by competing against yourself, preempts competitors by giving them less room to maneuver. Instead of competing with just one other brand, they have to position their products somewhere between the two that are already in the market.

Broader market for you

There is nothing wrong with producing a cheaper or more expensive version of your own product. It expands the appeal to other market segments that may be outside the range of your original product.

When viewers see two stair-climbing exercise gadgets competing against each other, it creates more awareness of stair-climbing as a method of exercise. Furthermore, the

> *note* If people bought your original product, your knock-off is likely to score the same success with its respective market segment.

competition creates the sense that the product is both a popular and effective way to exercise.

Soliciting a direct response

Infomercials and DRTV spots are both designed to solicit a specific response directly from TV viewers. What do you want the viewers to do? What do you want the viewers to get? These are the two fundamental questions your infomercial or DRTV spot must answer effectively.

 Regardless of which form of advertising you use, certain rules always apply:

- **Be explicit:** Tell the viewers exactly what you want them to do. Some advertisers get so engrossed highlighting the fantastic features of their product, they bury their solicitation message and fail to stress what they want the TV viewers to do.

- **Be direct:** Solicit a response that is direct—and measurable. If your objective is to get the consumers to visit their nearest shopping center to look for your product, this is not direct response advertising.

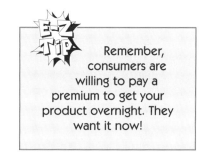

Remember, consumers are willing to pay a premium to get your product overnight. They want it now!

- **Be measurable:** The response must be quantifiable. Even if you're running a simple opinion poll, the response must be something that can be measured in a way that defines the success or failure of either the advertisement itself or of the product being advertised.

Leads or sales?

Infomercials and DRTV spots commonly solicit either a direct purchase or an inquiry about a product. Again, be explicit. don't give the viewer an option. If you do, your response mix will be inaccurate, confusing, and counterproductive.

 A *lead generation* infomercial or DRTV spot asks the viewers to call your toll-free 800 number and to leave their name and address to receive additional
DEFINITION sales information about your product or service.

DEFINITION

A *sales generation* infomercial or DRTV spot prompts the viewer paying by credit card or COD, to call your toll-free 800 number to place an order for your product or service.

Stick with a single response objective

Your infomercial that solicits viewers to make a direct purchase may also generate calls requesting additional information. Although these unsolicited calls must be treated as highly qualified leads, they cannot be used to measure the actual success of

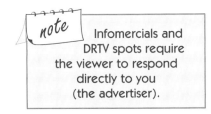

note

Infomercials and DRTV spots require the viewer to respond directly to you (the advertiser).

your infomercial. Since your principal objective is to generate direct dollar sales, all the calls that generated leads must be treated as windfall.

What happens when customers go to the store for your product?

Some consumers want to see a product before they purchase it. Others don't have a credit card or fail to note the ordering information provided in your infomercial.

This large contingent of potential customers can provide you with extra profits from retail sales generated by your infomercial or DRTV spot. For example, exercise machines like the Thigh Master and certain types of sunglasses, like Blu Blockers, enjoyed increased retail sales due to direct response advertising by the aggressive marketers of those products.

Create a trend

Direct response pioneers like *The Juice Man* and *The Juice Tiger* sold truckloads of juice extractors with their infomercials. These two competing brands, however, did more than sell juice machines on television—they

> **note** As a rule of thumb, infomercials and DRTV spots are designed to encourage retail sales 24-hours a day.

convinced consumers that juice was important and showed them how juice machines can help them lead healthier, happier lives.

Consequently, these infomercials helped the retail sales of almost every brand of juice maker. With their new awareness, consumers became receptive to the idea of owning a juice machine. Stores began merchandising juice machines, allocating prime store footage to display different brands. Without any new advertising effort, juice-making machine manufacturers now enjoy additional retail sales that were generated by The Juice Man and The Juice Tiger infomercials.

This example proves that an infomercial may effectively sell directly to a specific TV audience while simultaneously producing retail sales. You can see how retail sales can be generated without any additional

> **note** An increase in retail sales of a number of products has been directly attributed to infomercials or DRTV spots.

advertising expense—since the infomercial or DRTV spot which prompted the retail sales actually paid for itself through direct sales to TV viewers.

Outperforming retail sales

Moving consumers from conventional retail buying to direct response television buying is another triumph that demonstrates the power of an infomercial marketer.

Until recently, women bought cosmetics from department stores or *Avon*. Victoria Jackson began to sell complete systems exclusively through television infomercials. The only way customers could buy products was by responding to her paid TV programming.

Prior to Jackson's infomercial, 3 out of every 4 *Victoria Jackson* customers bought cosmetics exclusively from department stores. In response to Jackson's success, Avon is designing an infomercial campaign of its own.

A new form of advertising

Today's infomercials are a far cry from the "long-form" televised sales pitches (5- and 10-minute commercials) of the early '60s. This was when half-hour shows sponsored by soap manufacturers gave birth to the term "soap opera." TV advertising three decades ago was largely confined to promotions which:

- told viewers that a particular product with certain features existed

- motivated viewers to go to the nearest retail outlet to buy the product

- in the strict sense, was nothing but an advertising medium

Today, television has evolved from a mere advertising medium into a dominant distribution vehicle. Today's infomercials and direct response TV commercials go beyond product promotion. They actually give the consumer a means to directly purchase the merchandise being advertised.

note

98% of all U. S. households have at least one television set. TV has surpassed all other media as our primary source of information and entertainment.

Direct response marketing remained the domain of mail order and other print forms of direct marketing until television matured, and advertisers began to recognize its direct marketing potential. In fact, the terms *infomercial* and *DRTV spots* came into being because television gives the advertisers a platform conducive to direct marketing, at all hours of the day and night.

Since we've evolved from being a 9 to 5 society, television executives recognized the profitable viewership base found in late-night hours. With thousands of national, regional and local TV stations, and with extended programming hours, airtime is readily available. The growth of cable TV, satellites, and superstations has brought television a long way since the time when we only had CBS, NBC, and ABC.

The advantages of infomercials

- **Shopping without guilt.** Direct response television lets consumers shop without having to confront a salesperson. Buying from the tube eliminates any pressure on the consumer. The ability to shop hassle-free makes retail television an attractive alternative.

- **Time.** Regardless of the product, convenience is always a strong sales motivator. Nothing is more convenient than picking up the telephone to place an order.

- **Uniqueness.** Many products sold through direct response are not available through retail outlets. When they are, the DRTV version of the products will either have unique features (like no-smear lipstick), or carry substantially lower prices.

> *note*
> 60% of all TV households in the U. S. have cable service, providing a wide variety of channel selections.

- **Impact.** An audio-visual sales presentation is both compelling and convincing. Since department store salespeople are often unfamiliar with the uses, operation, and versatility of all their products, retail outlets consistently fail to get consumers excited about a product.

Canadian markets

The Canadian government passed new laws to clamp down on U.S. mail order and infomercial companies. The goal is to make it expensive and more difficult for Canadians to order from U.S. addresses. The ceiling on tax-free imports delivered by mail or courier will be increased from $20 to $40. The Canadians also have a $5 handling fee on any taxable parcel.

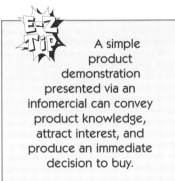

A simple product demonstration presented via an infomercial can convey product knowledge, attract interest, and produce an immediate decision to buy.

- **800 number access.** If your infomercial or DRTV spots airing in U.S. markets spill over to Canada, make sure your toll-free 800 number can be dialed from Canada. Be particularly concerned with superstations like WGN or WOR.

- **3% SHARE.** Your sales from Canadian TV viewers will depend on:

  ✦ the product you're selling

  ✦ the TV stations you use for your U.S. airings.

Some U.S. companies obtain as much as 3% of their total sales from Canada.

Producing your own infomercial

10

Chapter 10
Producing your own infomercial

Although most advertisers hire experienced production firms to develop, write and produce their infomercial campaigns, many entrepreneurs produce their own.

Self-managed, self-produced projects have become a popular option for a lot of advertisers because of relatively lower expenses, or the nature of the products themselves, or because the advertisers want creative control. Following are the main reasons why this is so:

- **Financial interest:** Some entrepreneurs don't want to share profits with partners or investors. But without them, most start-up companies do not have the capital to hire a full-service infomercial company.

- **Product appeal:** The entrepreneur's product is untested as an infomercial item, making it difficult to attract partners or investors.

• **Creative control:** Many entrepreneurs argue that they know more about their product than anyone else. They therefore prefer not to leave the creation of their infomercial to an outsider.

Three stages are normally involved in the creation and production of any infomercial or direct response TV campaign:

1) concept stage

2) production stage

3) media stage

The concept stage

In this section, we discuss what you need to know in formulating your direct response campaign. It assumes that you already know everything there is to know about your product, and that you believe your product will do well on TV, either because it has sold well elsewhere or because similar products are already doing well with DRTV.

Determine what you want

Certain fundamental questions should be answered before you continue: What do you want the viewers to do? What do you want to get out of your DRTV campaign? Do you want sales or leads? Are you better off with a lead generation DRTV spot or a sales generation infomercial?

Whatever type of response you decide upon, that response must meet these criteria:

• **Be explicit.** Tell the viewers exactly what you want them to do. Some advertisers bury their solicitation message. By becoming engrossed in highlighting the fantastic features of their product, they fail to stress what they want the TV viewers to do.

- **The response must be direct.** Provide your viewers with a direct response pipeline to you. Remember, an infomercial or DRTV spot that asks viewers to visit their nearest shopping center to look for your product is not direct response advertising. An infomercial or DRTV spot requires the viewer to respond directly to you.

- **The response must be measurable.** Even if you're running a simple opinion poll, you must be able to measure the response to determine the success or failure of your product or service.

Leads only

There are three practical reasons why you may prefer to produce a lead generating campaign as opposed to a sales generating one:

- **Product features are too complicated.** If the uses of your product cannot be described in a simple, entertaining manner, you will have serious problems with a sales generation DRTV campaign.

- **Several models.** If your product line contains a variety of models that may confuse the viewer, you're better off sending follow-up sales material that distinguishes the features of each model.

- **Costs over $100.** If you can sell a $500 item with a sales generation infomercial or one minute DRTV spot, go for it. But, you are an exception to the general rule that a DRTV product should cost no more than $100. (One exception to the rule is offering an installment payment plan. You'll learn more about that later.)

Two-step campaign

A lead generation DRTV spot or infomercial is always a prelude to direct mail campaign, hence the term *two-step* is applied to the use of a DRTV spot or infomercial to generate leads. The following usually takes place:

- **The viewer calls.** In a lead generation DRTV spot, you advertise a toll-free 800# for viewers to call to leave their name and address in order to get more information by mail. The calls are answered by live operators or by an automated voice-processing system.

- **You send sales information.** Brochures, videos, or other forms of sales material are sent to induce the recipient to place an order. Example: Nordic Track sends an impressive combination of a video and a booklet of their product lines to people who respond to their DRTV spot.

Dual-purpose campaigns

Lead generation advertising should usually be in the form of standard-length DRTV spots, not infomercials. If you have already decided to use an infomercial, at least offer the viewers the opportunity to make a direct purchase. This will offset the costs of production and media.

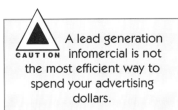
A lead generation infomercial is not the most efficient way to spend your advertising dollars.

If you do want to generate both actual sales and lead inquiries, be explicit about it. If you show only your 800 number order line, you may alienate people who want to call for additional information. On the other hand, if you ask for lead generation, you probably won't get any sales.

 If at all possible, have two telephone numbers: one for sales, one for inquiries.

Pricing

DRTV advertising should not dictate the price of your product, which must be identified before you start formulating your DRTV project. However, certain factors should be considered in determining the price of your product.

- **Economic value.** This factor has nothing to do with your manufacturing cost. It is the perceived value of your product based on the convenience or satisfaction it is likely to provide the consumer. A $100 toothbrush cleaner has little economic value, since a consumer would purchase a replacement toothbrush for $2 before investing $100 on a toothbrush cleaner.

- **Shipping and handling.** The consumer sees this as a cost added to the price of your product. You should view it as a way to pay not only shipping costs, but also your cost of order taking. Furthermore, where possible, upsell the buyer to order overnight delivery at a premium charge.

- **Payment plans.** Payment plans for credit card buyers come in a variety of packages, depending on the category and base price of the product. For products under $100, plans offering 3 payments are the most common. On the high-end of the spectrum, for example, an exercise machine has a plan offering 10 payments of $49.95.

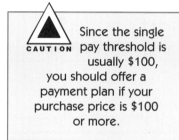

CAUTION Since the single pay threshold is usually $100, you should offer a payment plan if your purchase price is $100 or more.

Several studies indicate that the number of infomercials offering payment plans have increased threefold over the last two years.

Creating urgency

Try to create a sense of urgency by offering an incentive. No matter how good your product is, no matter how low the price, offering a bonus is an old strategy that usually works like a charm. Bonuses entice viewers to purchase immediately.

- **TV price.** You may offer a special TV price lower than the regular retail price of your product.

- **Price break.** This technique is usually effective for consumables. You can offer a 50% discount on additional quantities of the product purchased at the same time.

- **Free product.** Offer a special item free to those who purchase through your special TV offer.

Production of your infomercial

To begin with, an infomercial is usually a half-hour in length, and there will be significant expense for production.

The right format is at the heart of every infomercial project. Your production cost, the way you present your information, the pacing of your show, and its ability to keep the audience glued to the TV depends on your infomercial's format.

Following are two examples of effective formats: *Time-Life* produced its *"Rock 'N Roll of the '60s"* infomercial as a music video documentary hosted by a disc jockey who presents a succession of music videos from a broadcast control booth. *Psychic Friends Network* made its infomercial a talk show hosted by Dionne Warwick before a live audience.

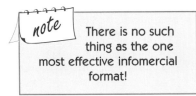

There is no such thing as the one most effective infomercial format!

Shoot your infomercial in a format that best demonstrates the benefits of your product. Having a roomful of people with serious bald spots may not be the most aesthetically pleasing sight on television. However, it was certainly the most effective way for Ron Popiel to introduce his GLH Formula, a baldness treatment.

If you're having trouble deciding between different formats, watching some of the most popular regular TV programs may offer some interesting clues. One thing to think about is what your viewers are accustomed to watching on television today. One example of popular programming is tabloid-type programs like *A Current Affair, Rescue 911,* and *Hard Copy.* These shows present investigative segments which explore specific subjects in an exciting and entertaining manner.

Rules of scripting

Once you've established your primary objective and decided on a format, it's time to write your infomercial.

Rule 1: Prepare an outline for a script writer. Explain what your product is, its use, its user benefits, and its economic value.

> ⚠ **CAUTION** Unless you're an experienced writer who can create a fast-paced, well-staged, logically arranged, audio-visual sales presentation, don't even try writing your infomercial.

Rule 2: If you think you possess the inherent talent to write out your own presentation, keep this in mind: You're not there to look cute or impress your competitors with how creative you are. Focus on the product.

When writing your infomercial script, every word must draw blood!

NEVER STOP SELLING! Remember, if the TV viewer does not reach for the phone to place an order, it won't work.

Keep it interesting. With the advent of remote control, your infomercial must be engaging. You may have a potentially good product, but if you cannot hold the viewer's attention, the remote control is your worst enemy.

Blockscripting

DEFINITION

An infomercial is divided into several smaller segments that are usually repeated within the half-hour show. This is a result of infomercial writers using *block scripting* (also known as *pocket scripting*) for an infomercial.

When preparing your outline, imagine a channel hopper landing on your infomercial at any given part. You have about 60 seconds to give this viewer an idea of what you're selling to keep him interested. If you fail to keep that viewer's attention, you just lost a potential sale. A fast-paced script will keep your viewer watching.

As a rule of thumb, to keep an infomercial interesting, something entertaining and informative must be happening every 60 seconds.

Scripting checklist

Decide which of the following elements will make up the core of your presentation. These ingredients will influence the style of your show and the manner in which your product will be presented to your TV audience:

- *Testimonials.* This format presents satisfied customers talking about their successful experiences with your product. You can have actual product endorsers, or you can hire paid performers to do dramatized endorsements.

- *Interviews.* If you choose to include this format in your infomercial, you must decide whether the interview will be done as a panel (with a moderator) or one-on-one (an interviewer with one question at a time). Will the interview be in a studio or on location?

- *Celebrity endorsements.* A celebrity can add credibility and recognition to your product. A familiar face can make channel hoppers stop and watch your infomercial. Effectively used, a celebrity can be a wise investment. (See section on celebrities.)

- *Case histories.* A product with a demonstrable before-and-after effect, such as diet plans, cosmetics and fitness products, can provide a compelling argument for your product.

- *Demonstrations.* If your product's primary selling features are convenience and ease-of-use, you must capitalize on product demonstration as the backbone of your presentation.

- *Ordering information.* This segment usually lasts 30 to 45 seconds, informing the viewer of the product's price, accessories, tie-in items, bonuses, and refund guarantees that come with each order. It shows how the product is packaged and gives the delivery options available. It can be integrated into the DRTV spot or is presented independently.

- *DRTV spot.* This is usually a 2-minute spot that summarizes vital points about your product and the ordering procedure. To emphasize important points, most effective DRTV spots use footage lifted from the infomercial itself. The spot should be repeated at least 3 times within the infomercial.

Using celebrities

Using a famous face to sell your not-yet-famous product can be quite effective. It's one of the oldest tricks in the book, probably as old as television itself.

If you can afford it, using a celebrity, a recognized face, or a high-profile person can greatly increase sales of your product. A celebrity lends credibility to a product or service.

Consumers are more likely to be persuaded to accept a product they see used or endorsed by someone they know. A famous face can stop a channel hopper who may be curious to see what that celebrity is talking about. A celebrity can easily increase the viewing value of an infomercial.

Choosing a celebrity

Who should you get and why? That's the starting point of any celebrity search. How are you going to use the celebrity in your marketing campaign? Will the celebrity be a spokesperson or an endorser? Here's a checklist to consider:

DEFINITION

- **Appropriateness.** Telly Savalas was an effective endorser for the Player's Club, but would have been suicide for a hair care product! Believability is a key factor.

- **Spokesperson or endorser?** Decide which role the celebrity will play. A spokesperson is someone who interviews customers who have used the product being advertised. Someone presented as a customer who has actually used the product is an endorser.

- **Support all claims.** Advertisers must provide documentation to support all celebrity claims made whether as a spokesperson or endorser.

- **Insurance and indemnification.** Celebrities acting as endorsers may seek protection against possible lawsuits. He or she may demand that an advertiser maintain product liability insurance naming the celebrity as an additionally insured party. They almost always require indemnification from the advertiser.

Costs of celebrity acquisitions may be determined using one of the two following compensation packages:

1) a guaranteed fee with back-end participation

2) a straight buyout

Guarantee and participation

With a guarantee, you will be required to pay the celebrity an up-front fee plus a percentage of your gross or net sales. The *up-front guarantee* can range anywhere from $5,000 to $20,000. The back-end percentage may be between 1% and 5% of either your gross or your net sales.

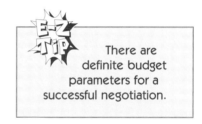

There are definite budget parameters for a successful negotiation.

In this type of compensation package, however, the celebrity's guarantee fee is actually part of the back-end participation. The guaranteed fee is actually a deductible advance guarantee which is subtracted from the cumulative value of the back-end percentage.

For example: You hire Celeb X for a guarantee fee of $10,000 plus 5% of your gross receipts over a campaign period of one year. If you generate gross sales of $500,000, Celeb X's total participation fee will amount to $25,000.

However, since you already advanced $10,000, you will only owe the difference of $15,000 at the end of the year.

DEFINITION

A *straight buyout* compensation package that is a one-time fee you pay a celebrity for appearing in your infomercial. Among other factors, the length of time you want to use the infomercial and its geographic distribution (local, regional, or national) will determine how much you pay.

Celebs: perks & more

The basic compensation package is usually just the beginning of the negotiation process. The following factors are equally critical to a celebrity who is evaluating your acquisition offer:

- **Length & exclusivity.** Celebrities usually don't want to be contractually bound for long periods of time. Most agreements are for one year with options to renew. Exclusivity is also crucial. It prohibits the celebrity from endorsing or acting as a spokesperson for a competing product.

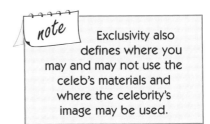

note Exclusivity also defines where you may and may not use the celeb's materials and where the celebrity's image may be used.

- **Related media.** If the celeb's appeal is strong enough to make a significant difference in your product's appeal, use him or her in your print ads, sales literature, or even your packaging. Although this usually requires more work for the celebrity, the perceived value of his/her participation in your overall marketing campaign will definitely mean more dollars in the compensation package.

- **Transportation & accommodation.** Since most celebrities belong to a union, you will be required to hire them under union terms. This means first-class air travel and accommodation wherever you are shooting your infomercial. If the celeb demands to bring a companion, the perks should be extended.

Try the agencies below for celebrity brokering, or contact your local agencies:

- Celebrity Endorsement Network—(818) 704-6709

- Ingles, Inc.—(213) 464-0800

- Jack King Celeb Brokers—(310) 652-5700

STAR GUIDE—This is a trade-size directory of over 3,000 names and addresses of TV and movie stars, musicians, sports celebrities, politicians, and other famous people. Updated every year. Complete alphabetical index. Over 175 pages. $14.95 Published by Axiom Information Resources, P.O. Box 8015 Ann Arbor, MI 48107 . . . http://www.celebritylocator.com

Shooting your infomercial

You can write your own script and direct the actual shooting of your infomercial, but you should never shoot and edit your own infomercial unless you have all the necessary equipment and know-how.

During the actual shoot stage, all the footage that will form part of your infomercial is shot. Your responsibilities should focus on selecting and hiring the camera crew.

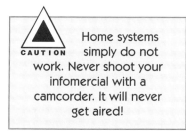

CAUTION Home systems simply do not work. Never shoot your infomercial with a camcorder. It will never get aired!

After all the footage is shot, you enter the post-production phase. It is time to edit your infomercial, taking out the bad cuts and putting all the good shots into one coherent presentation, adding music and special effects, and more. During this stage, you will be responsible for selecting and hiring a post-production facility with the right editing system and a competent editor.

Use the same company to shoot your infomercial and do all the editing and post-production work for three reasons:

1) The post-production people are already familiar with your project and how it was shot.

2) Rates are usually cheaper for a packaged deal

3) If you worry about confidentiality, you'll only have one supplier to worry about.

Choosing a tape format

If you have the money and demand the highest quality, shoot your infomercial on film rather than on videotape. You will have more flexibility and the highest quality post-production effects available.

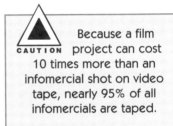

Chances are the production company you hire will try to convince you that the best tape format is the one they have in their studio. Those who use Beta will tell you Beta is the best. Those who use 8mm will tell you about the miracles it can do. If you shop around, you are likely to hear the advantages and disadvantages of every format there is.

- **Betacam.** This is currently the favored video format because it delivers the highest video resolution. Since Beta equipment is expensive, expect to pay more to shoot in this format. The popularity of Beta mastering tapes is disturbing, since no TV stations require Beta as an actual broadcast copy tape. All in all, the Beta format is overrated because it is not used at the television stations themselves. (Average daily rental of a Beta-Cam with camera crew—$995)

    > ⚠ **CAUTION** Because a film project can cost 10 times more than an infomercial shot on video tape, nearly 95% of all infomercials are taped.

- **3/4-Inch U-Matic.** If you want basic broadcast quality at a good price, use 3/4-Inch U-Matic. You can shoot and edit without having to change formats, and you can make same format dubbed copies of your finished master for broadcast copy. (Average daily rental with camera crew—$495)

- **S-VHS.** This is a higher grade VHS with 400-line resolution. Although not particularly recommended as a "finishing" format, it works perfectly for non-sensitive outdoor shoots. If you're shooting testimonials from different locations, S-VHS will provide portability and acceptable quality. (Average daily rental with camera crew—$295)

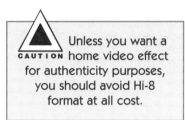

Unless you want a home video effect for authenticity purposes, you should avoid Hi-8 format at all cost.

- **HI-8**. Some production outfits build their system around this 3-chip Hi-8 camera format. In spite of its impressive specifications, Hi-8 has inherent shortcomings.

- **1-Inch.** Whereas all the previous formats are in cassette form, 1-inch tapes come in reel form. Since most cameras and editing systems are not built around the 1-inch format, it is never used for production, but primarily for broadcast copy. Whether you shoot your infomercial in Beta, U-Matic, or S-VHS format, you may need to dub your finished master into a 1-inch copy for airing with some TV stations. (Average cost of 1-inch dub copy—$100.)

Finished length

From the first frame to the last, your infomercial should be 28 minutes and 30 seconds long. Your first frame should actually be the standard disclaimer stating that "this is a paid program" from your company. Your last frame should state that "the preceding was a paid program" presented by your company.

Post-production

Post-production is the part of the production process where you create the tone of your infomercial, so we'll review what's involved.

Post-production is usually considered the editing stage, although it involves much more than just editing footage. Text, graphics, background music, and video and audio effects are all added during post-production.

note With today's technology, your infomercial's ultimate look is limited only by your imagination and your budget.

How you cut, fade-in, fade-out, insert, roll, and merge one scene with the next lends to the overall tempo of your show. This is where you can run wild with animation, 3-D graphics, split screen, multi-screen, and much more.

For rock-bottom, basic post-production work, you can use a studio with a system built around a desktop video system. Popular desktop brands like Video Toasters and Matrox will give you basic broadcast quality (average rate—$75 per hour) integrated simultaneously in a variety of ways, using a wide assortment of effects. Although some companies using desktop-level video editing systems have A-B roll capability, most post-production houses with this capability use more sophisticated, top-of-the line editing systems. (Average rate—$125 per hour.)

DEFINITION

The future of post-production is *non-linear editing*, called this because your program is edited without using a tape. Instead, the hard drives of the computer store and manipulate the images you've shot. The system is highly digital and usually comes loaded with effects. And since it edits at the speed of a digital hard drive, your work is finished faster and with more creative flair. (Average rate—$250 per hour.)

TV order slates

DEFINITION

Whether you are using infomercials or regular DRTV spots, you are limited to a few seconds to give your audience information on how and where to place their orders. This segment is called an *order slate*.

Order slates contain information about your name, address and telephone number as it appears on the TV screen. Here are a few tips on how to effectively design your order slate:

Toll-free 800 numbers

 If you do not have the capacity to handle multiple simultaneous calls, you need to hire a service bureau to handle order taking.

Most infomercial source companies have affiliations with their own service bureaus to provide order taking service. Because the service bureaus have special arrangements with your source company, their rates are usually lower, making them a favorable choice.

If you decide to go with your source company's service bureau, make sure they are willing to:

1) Give you your own unique 800 number.

2) Give you call reports on a daily basis.

3) Give you a copy of the itemized call statement from the phone company at the end of each month.

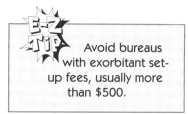
Avoid bureaus with exorbitant set-up fees, usually more than $500.

If you decide to hire your own service bureaus, shop around for the best rates. Make sure the bureau has the capability and the experience to handle your requirements, and that they operate 24 hours a day.

Business name

A standard order slate will show your 800 number along with your business name and mailing address. Remember that a TV viewer will have to copy all this information in order to write a check and mail it to the correct address. So make your wording short, clear, and easy to spell.

If your business name is long or complicated, you may want to open a new bank account using a different name. Acronyms usually work best. For example, if your business name is Communicators International Enterprises, register a new account for C.I.E. Both you and your customers will benefit from such a change.

Mailing address

Since mailing addresses appear on the TV screen for just a few seconds, post office box numbers or short addresses are easier to remember and spell.

For example, if your business is in a city named *Lauderdale-By-The-Sea*, you might want to drive a few miles south to get a P.O. box in Miami. It's not only more recognizable, but it is shorter and easier for viewers to spell.

More media tips

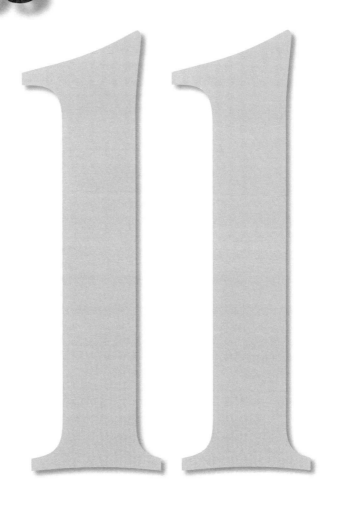

Chapter 11

More media tips

From an economic standpoint, media is the most important stage in your infomercial project because it involves the largest chunk of your budget. How you buy your TV airtime dictates the profitability of your direct response campaign. Buy poorly, and you can lose a fortune.

E-Z TIP

If you buy your TV airtime wisely, you can make a fortune.

Our discussion of media buying will be based on half-hour infomercials. Unless specified otherwise, figures, stats, and examples used in this chapter will be for half-hour, sales generation infomercials.

Besides actual media buying, product fulfillment and other activities generally associated with the media stage of your infomercial campaign will be considered.

State of television

When the American TV viewing market was being served by only three or four stations—ABC, CBS, NBC, and in some cities, an independent station—behavioral and social patterns were mainstream and demographic diversity was not an issue. Viewing patterns were, therefore, quite similar everywhere. Back then, media buying was relatively easy.

Now the reverse is true. With cable service, satellite programming, low-power and full-power broadcasting, the route to today's TV audiences is more complicated and difficult to follow.

Fortunately, television retailing pioneers have paved part of the way for us, making it possible to identify certain media-buying styles that work well for infomercials.

> *note* Today, the U.S. TV viewing public is divided into over 200 markets, each with 20 to 30 channels to choose from.

For example, those who cultivated DRTV have proven to us that buying late-night TV time is cost effective. Since late-night airtime costs less, it delivers one of the lowest *cost per order,* or *CPO,* figures obtained, enabling marketers to break even with fewer orders.

There are three types of commercial TV stations, distinguished by how their programming is delivered to the public—broadcast, cable and superstations.

Broadcast

Broadcast TV stations use the airwaves to transmit their programs over a specific geographic area. By design, all broadcast stations are local, to the extent the power of their antennas transmit their signals to TV viewers. Some broadcast TV channels are also carried by the local cable service in the station's primary broadcast area.

Based on their transmitting power, there are two types of broadcast TV stations:

1) low power, usually operating on UHF frequencies

2) full power, those you usually get as channels 2 through 13 if you don't have cable. These depend on your antenna to pick up the TV signals.

The four most recognized broadcast TV networks in the U.S. are ABC, CBS, NBC, and FOX. It is difficult, if not impossible, to acquire TV airtime on any of these networks. With the possible exception of Ross Perot's half-hour paid announcements during his '92 presidential election bid, no half-hour paid programs are aired on the broadcast network level. On a local level, however, network affiliates have different policies regarding paid programming.

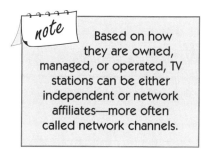

note Based on how they are owned, managed, or operated, TV stations can be either independent or network affiliates—more often called network channels.

Cable

Cable stations are TV stations whose programming is delivered exclusively through a cable system, meaning homes without cable service have no way of watching these channels. Since these stations send their signals to different cable service companies across the country, they are also referred to as networks. The extent of the coverage of any cable network depends entirely on the number of local cable service companies carrying its programming.

The following are the 10 most widely distributed basic cable networks. Figures are in total million households.

Cable Network	Call Letters	Million Households
Cable News Network	CNN	66
Cable News & Business	CNBC	65
USA Network	USA	65
Video Hits	VH1	64
Nickelodeon	NIK	63
Lifetime	LIFE	61
Headline News	HLN	61
Entertainment Sports	ESPN	61
Discovery	DSC	61
Music Television	MTV	61

Superstations

DEFINITION

A *superstation* is a local broadcast station whose programming is being received by cable markets outside its primary broadcast area. Without the cable aspect of their coverage, they are nothing more than local broadcast TV stations. Without the broadcast aspect of their coverage, they are strictly a cable channel.

A regional superstation has its programming carried by cable companies within the same state or region where the superstation operates. Examples include WPIX in Florida and KTVT in Texas.

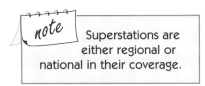
note
Superstations are either regional or national in their coverage.

A national superstation has its programming carried by cable companies in more than one state. The three major national superstations are TNT, WOR, and WGN.

Georgia-based TNT, part of the Turner Broadcasting Group, is known for programming dominated by its extensive collection of old movies. TBS also has strict guidelines on direct response programming and rarely accepts paid programs. WOR and WGN have a more enterprising position. They have extensive market coverage and their rates are extremely competitive.

Superstations	Subscribers (per million)
WWOR	35
WWGN	42
WPIX	12
KTVT	4

Top TV markets

Television, both broadcast and cable, reaches over 93 million homes in over 200 major U.S. markets. Sixty-three million have cable service. The 10 largest TV markets in the U.S., with a total of 26.6 million homes (28% of all viewing homes) are:

TV market	TV Households	% homes w/cable
New York	7.0	58
Los Angeles	5.0	57
Chicago	3.1	77
Philadelphia	2.7	70
San Francisco	2.2	64
Boston	2.1	71
Washington, D.C.	1.7	57
Dallas-Ft. Worth	1.7	47
Detroit	1.7	59
Houston	1.5	50

Media joint ventures

Entering into a joint venture with a TV station simply means that the station is willing to extend you the airtime in exchange for a percentage of your sales. Or, they will finance you for a flat fee based on units sold or inquiries generated during each airing.

> **note**
> Purchasing television airtime requires a substantial amount of upfront capital. It is therefore common to seek joint ventures to finance your media buys.

Since TV stations rarely advertise this aspect of their business, you may have to call a number of them to find those who accept *per order* (PO) or *per inquiry* (PI) deals.

There are also media brokers who put together similar deals. Service bureaus who broker turnkey infomercial projects also have access to TV stations that will do PO/PI deals.

Regardless of which route you take, you will be required to produce customized material that shows an 800 number exclusive to the TV station on which your material is being aired. This will allow both you and the station to track the number of leads or sales generated by each airing.

Per inquiry

If you have a lead generation DRTV spot, some TV stations, particularly those with huge inventories of unsold commercial time, will accept payment based on the actual number of leads each airing of your ad generates.

Per inquiry deals are usually confined to 1- and 2-minute DRTV spots. TV stations seldom extend half-hour airtime for a lead-generation infomercial. If they do, however, expect to pay a premium for each inquiry you generate with each airing.

Some stations may require a guarantee to run your DRTV spot on a per inquiry basis. For example, if you agree to spend $1 for each inquiry, the station may require you to give them $300 in advance until you've generated the equivalent of 300 leads.

Per order

Per order deals are usually available for both DRTV spots and half-hour infomercials. With per order advertising, the station may charge a fixed amount for each unit sold or a percentage—between 30% and 75%—of the gross value of the product.

As with per inquiry deals, some stations may want a guarantee before they air your infomercial or DRTV spot. The guaranteed amount is usually based on the percentage the station expects to earn from the selling price of your product.

For example, if your product sells for $100 and the station wants 50%, the station will want a guarantee based on $50 per unit. If the station asks for $1,000 as a guarantee, it will run your infomercial or DRTV spot until you've sold 20 units.

Buying on CPO

If your media buys are to be based on a single common denominator that monitors performance, it should be *Cost Per Order* (CPO).

The lower your CPO, the higher your profits. Remember, with DRTV, media buying has nothing to do with programming or demographics. It is strictly a numbers game. The fewer dollars you spend to reach your viewer base, the better your CPO.

CPO should generally be under 50% of selling price. To determine your CPO, simply divide your airtime cost by the number of orders you generated from that single airing of your infomercial. This amount should be less that 50% of your selling price.

> *note*
>
> In direct response television, the bottom line is your CPO— how much it costs you to generate one sale or one inquiry.

Performance ratio

DEFINITION *Performance ratio* is a percentage derived from dividing your CPO by your selling price, or by dividing your total sales revenue by your total media cost.

Although the maximum CPO should be 50% of your selling price, few advertisers consider 50% to be acceptable. Ideally, your CPO should be 1/5 your selling price, which means you should receive $5 for every dollar you invest in media.

For example, if $1,000 worth of airtime produces 50 sales, your CPO is $20, which means it costs you $20 in media time to sell one unit of your product.

- If your selling price is $40, your CPO is 50% of your selling price ($20 divide $40), a 1 to 2 ratio.

- If your selling price is $60, your CPO is 33% of your selling price ($20 divide $60), a 1 to 3 ratio.

- If your selling price is $100, your CPO is 20% of your selling price ($20 divide $100), a 1 to 5 ratio. This means that for every dollar you invest in media time, you're getting $5 back.

Monitoring & evaluation

 The success or failure of an infomercial can be determined by one or two airings. If the first airing produces marginal results, you may want to give it a second shot for comparison. If the second airing is equally disappointing, go back to the drawing board.

Immediately evaluate the performance of each airing the morning after. Although orders may continue to straggle in two or three days after an infomercial is aired, each airing's performance can be largely determined by evaluating it within 12 hours.

Each airing must be profitable—no ifs, ands, or buts.
Your only other concern should be to compare the
CPO and ratio of one media buy to the next.

Infomercials are not like regular programs, which, with metered frequency, can build viewership. If your infomercial does not deliver a profitable return after one or two airings, it probably never will.

Furthermore, if after one or two airings, your infomercial proves profitable, your next task is to develop a media plan to increase those profits. By selecting stations, time slots, and air dates that will produce the lowest CPOs, you can dramatically increase your profit ratio.

Types of media buys

To appreciate the true value of a particular media buy, we grouped TV stations into three categories and analyzed their rates based on their comparative coverage. The three categories are:

1) **National.** These TV stations are either cable networks or national super-stations. (To illustrate, we'll use Nickelodeon at 1:30 a.m. on weekdays at a cost of $12,500.)

2) **Primary.** These are local broadcast TV stations in major cities with at least one million TV homes. (We'll use WPGH, the FOX affiliate in Pittsburgh, at 1:30 a.m. on weekdays with a cost of $900.)

3) **Secondary.** These are local broadcast TV stations in smaller or secondary cities, with usually less than 500,000 TV homes. (We'll use WWAT, an independent in Columbus, Ohio, at 1:30 a. m. on weekdays with a cost of $150.)

Charting comparative rates and effective reach of each station yields the following:

TV group	Rate	TV homes	CPM
Nationals	$12,500	63 million	0.20
Primary	$900	1.2 million	0.75
Secondary	$150	350,000	0.43

DEFINITION

CPM stands for "cost per thousand" (M stands for Mil, Latin for thousand). Based on the preceding table, if all the potential viewers being reached by each respective station were watching that station at that time, it would cost 20 cents to reach every 1,000 viewers watching a widely subscribed cable network, 75 cents for a primary station, and 43 cents in a secondary market.

Although it seems obvious that you may want to split your media buys between the national and secondary markets, often this is not possible. Airtime on national stations is hard to come by. Fewer than 20 cable networks and superstations fall into this category, and most available infomercial time has already been purchased or is controlled by major media brokers and infomercial production houses.

Finding good secondary markets involves a fair amount of research. It is best to deal with media brokers who specialize in this category.

Testing

In the test market stage, it is unwise to invest a lot in national media buys. It is better to spread your budget over a string of secondary markets to get a better feel for viewer feedback.

DEFINITION

Always test media on an *OTO* (*one-time-only*) basis. Even Fortune 500 companies with multi-million dollar budgets always test their products and the media where they

>
> As soon as the first draft of your infomercial is completed, make several copies and send one to each station you are considering.

are placed. No one can accurately predict the outcome of an untested campaign. Lay out a sensible test campaign and evaluate the results accordingly.

For do-it-yourselfers, secondary markets with airtime rates between $150 and $400 offer low-risk vehicles for test marketing your infomercial. Although TV stations in secondary markets do not generally offer the best CPM (compare to nationwide cable channels), they charge the lowest entry fees required to get a fair "let-the-market-decide" type of evaluation of an infomercial.

Approval

Before you send any tape for approval, contact the station to confirm that they have available airtime. The approval process can take anywhere from a day to a month, depending on who you know and the overall attitude at that station.

Media brokers

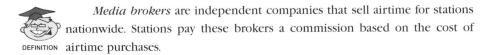

DEFINITION *Media brokers* are independent companies that sell airtime for stations nationwide. Stations pay these brokers a commission based on the cost of airtime purchases.

Brokers come in all shapes and sizes, depending on the type of TV stations they represent and their volume of business. In some cases, brokers who buy a lot of media time have better pricing leverage. Therefore, two brokers may have different rates for the same time slot at the same station.

Brokers: a one-stop shop for TV airtime

Brokers are particularly helpful when you're buying airtime on a network affiliate (ABC, CBS, NBC, FOX), a cable network (ESPN, A&E, CNN), or a superstation (WGN or WOR). Brokers give you access to as many stations in as many regions as you want, but you only have to deal with one person, saving you the hassle of negotiating with each station individually.

However, if you are buying airtime from stations in your city or in a familiar geographic area, using a broker may hurt rather than help. For

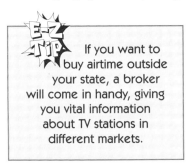

If you want to buy airtime outside your state, a broker will come in handy, giving you vital information about TV stations in different markets.

example, if the station you want to use does not recognize your broker, that broker may try to convince you to advertise on a station that will pay his commission.

Likewise, a media broker may cost you more if you are buying large quantities of airtime. By placing your order as a direct account, you can negotiate a rebate on the portion of the fee that the station would otherwise pay a broker.

Targeting by ZIP code

If your media buy is sensitive to demographics, one method of buying will be more precise, especially if you buy from local cable service companies.

 **note** The 5 digits of your ZIP code can tell a marketer what you ate for breakfast.

From Beverly Hills to the Bronx, expanding your geographic exposure is as easy as qualifying the socio-economic profiles of the audience. Marketers now use ZIP codes to identify the geographic distribution of their potential viewers. As markets become more segmented, a new method of categorizing American neighborhoods is gaining ground.

The Clustering of America, a book by Michael J. Weiss, dissected different lifestyles in America based on the U.S. Postal Service's *Zone Improvement Plan*—better known as ZIP code. *The Clustered World* by Weiss will expand on this concept through the next decade.

Weiss explained that your ZIP code, which actually represents the community where you live, reveals a lot about the people who live within its boundaries. The 5 digits of your ZIP code are being used to tell marketers the kinds of magazines you read, what you eat for breakfast, and the brand of toothpaste you are likely to use. Marketers are even using ZIP codes to decide what kind of celebrity to use in their advertising.

Joint-venture projects

 note Financing is a common roadblock for most start-up businesses; particularly if the business involves direct response television, which people outside the industry perceive as extremely high risk.

Infomercials, a relatively new form of marketing, have their share of critics who suspect their stability. Because of this—and the volatility of television—generally conventional financing is often out of the question.

A simple infomercial with no celebrities, elaborate props, or post-production effects may cost anywhere from $10,000 to $15,000 to shoot and edit in 3/4 inch U-Matic format.

Add to this another $10,000 to $15,000 for TV airtime, and you are looking at a minimum of $20,000 to reasonably launch an infomercial campaign on your own.

Infomercial marketing companies (IMCs)

Infomercial marketing companies (IMCs) are among the best sources for financing for two primary reasons:

- they are familiar with the industry and have available funds

- their hands-on involvement with your campaign provides helpful expertise.

Airtime inventory. The strength of IMCs lies in their huge inventory of excellent TV airtime available for half-hour paid programs. Most of these companies buy huge blocks of strategic (early evenings and weekends) airtime from most major cable networks.

> *note*
>
> Start-up businesses and individual entrepreneurs often seek friends and family members to provide seed capital for infomercial production and test marketing.

Quality production. Most IMCs have their own production facilities. Those who don't usually have access to the best production houses in the country. These production capabilities are usually combined with talent agencies that enable them to negotiate the best rates for celebrities.

Management. The third benefit to using an IMC is its experience in managing infomercial campaigns. If a major IMC takes on your product, your campaign is likely be handled by a team of experienced managers.

Proven products only

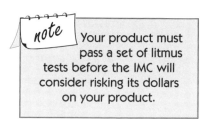

note Your product must pass a set of litmus tests before the IMC will consider risking its dollars on your product.

Two major constraints are normally imposed by IMCs. One has to do with your product—IMCs do not take on every product that comes their way. Presenting your product to an IMC is like an author selling his manuscript to a major publishing firm.

If you have only a prototype of your product, it may be more difficult to sell to an IMC. If the IMC does buy it, it usually gets involved with the actual manufacturing of your product.

Conversely, if your product has been successfully sold in some other form of direct response marketing, or if you have already produced and test marketed some version of your infomercial and have impressive sales performance numbers, IMCs will be more receptive. Furthermore, having numbers to substantiate your offer will give you negotiating leverage.

Control

Some entrepreneurs hesitate to deal with an IMC because of the control factor, both financial and creative. Without any numbers to back your projections, your figures are mere speculation.

As a newcomer to the business, you will not have the leverage to dictate financial terms nor will you have a free hand in determining how your product should be presented.

As with most other businesses, the leverage goes to the party with the most to offer. If you are new in the business and have an unproven product, you do not have the luxury of shopping around for the best offer. On the other hand, if you have a proven product, particularly one that has been test marketed via an infomercial, you can compare offers and negotiate the best terms.

Open deal

There is no set structure for financial terms between entrepreneurs and IMCs. Each company has a formula for structuring a deal, which may vary from one product to the next.

You will be better off focusing your evaluation on two factors:

1) How much money you stand to make based on their projections

2) How much time it will take for you to make your first dollar

Needless to say, where profit projections are concerned, IMCs tend to be conservative. When your objective is to convince them that your product will make them a lot of money, the IMC will naturally argue the opposite. Therefore, when evaluating an offer, consider your own projections objectively while viewing the IMC's figures as pessimistic.

Going upscale

To provide leverage for dealing with major IMCs, entrepreneurs commonly launch their own small scale infomercial campaigns to produce performance figures favorable for negotiation.

The strategy usually follows this sequence:

• You produce a simple infomercial to test market your product.

- You buy airtime in a number of secondary markets and track the results.

- You present your product and your test market numbers to an IMC.

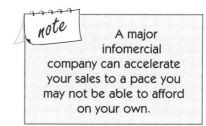

A major infomercial company can accelerate your sales to a pace you may not be able to afford on your own.

With a heftier production budget and a huge inventory of prime infomercial airtime, an IMC can do wonders for your campaign. You can reshoot your basic infomercial to feature celebrities and give your new infomercial a glossy look. And, with the expanded access to better TV airtime, your sales can soar at a rate you may not have been able to produce on your own.

Resources

••• Online Resources •••

◆ **AdRatecard**

http://www.adratecard.com/index.htm

◆ **Advertising and Marketing Helper**

http://www.geocities.com/WallStreet/3584/index2.html

◆ **Advertising Age magazine**

http://www.adage.com

◆ **AltaVista Small Business, Business Services, Marketing & PR**

http://altavista.looksmart.com/eus1/eus65300/eus65317/eus668 94/r?l&izf&

◆ **American Advertising Federation**

http://www.aaf.org

◆ **American Marketing Association**

http://www.ama.org

◆ **Association of National Advertisers, Inc.**

http://www.ana.net/default.htm

◆ **Celebrity Locator**

http://www.celebritylocator.com

◆ **Direct Marketing Association**

http://www.the-dma.org

◆ **Entertainment Resources & Marketing Association (ERMA)**

http://www.erma.org

◆ **Entrepreneur Magazine: Marketing 101**

http://www.entrepreneurmag.com/page.hts?N=989&Ad=S

◆ **Infomercial Index**

http://www.magickeys.com/infomercials/index.html

http://www.infomercialindex.com

◆ **Infoseek: Small Business**

http://infoseek.go.com/Center/Business/Small_business

◆ **International Association of Business Communicators**

http://www.iabc.com/homepage.htm

◆ **Internet Advertising Bureau**

http://www.iab.net

◆ **Lycos Directory: Small Business**

http://dir.lycos.com/Business/Small_Business

◆ **NetMarketing**

http://www.netb2b.com

◆ **Public Relations Society of America**

http://www.prsa.org

◆ **Showcase Placements, Inc.**

http://www.showcaseplacements.com/

◆ **SRDS**

http://www.srds.com/

◆ **Television Infomercials Directory by HandiLinks**

http://www.handilinks.com/cat1/t/16055.htm

◆ **U.S. Business Advisor**

URL: http://www.business.gov

◆ **Webcrawler: Small Business**

http://quicken.webcrawler.com/small_business

◆ **Yahoo! Business and Economy: News and Media**

http://dir.yahoo.com/Business_and_Economy/Companies/News_and_Media

◆ **Yahoo! News and Media: News and Media: Infomercials**

http://dir.yahoo.com/News_and_Media/Television/Commercials/Infomercials

◆ **Yahoo! Business & Economy: Informercials**

http://dir.yahoo.com/business_and_economy/companies/marketing/advertising/television/infomercials

◆ **Yahoo! Business and Economy: Production**

http://dir.yahoo.com/Business_and_Economy/Companies/Entertainment/Movies_and_Film/Production

◆ **Yahoo! Small Business**

http://smallbusiness.yahoo.com

◆ **ZineZone.com-Advertising**

http://www.zinezone.com/zines/wealth/industries/advertising/index.html

••• Related Sites •••

◆ **AOL.COM Business & Careers**

http://www.aol.com/webcenters/workplace/home.adp

◆ **BizMove.com**

http://www.bizmove.com

◆ **Biztalk.com Small Business Community**

http://www.biztalk.com

◆ **Bplans.com!**

http://www.bplans.com

◆ **BusinessTown.Com**

http://www.businesstown.com

◆ **Council of Better Business Bureaus, Inc.**

http://www.bbb.org

◆ **Education Index, Business Resources**

http://www.educationindex.com/bus

◆ **Electric Library® Business Edition**

http://www.business.elibrary.com

◆ **HotBot Directory/Small Business**

http://directory.hotbot.com/Business/Small_Business

◆ **Inc. Online**

http://www.inc.com

◆ **National Small Business United**

http://www.nsbu.org

◆ **Service Core of Retired Executives**

http://www.score.org

◆ **Small Business Advisor**

http://www.isquare.com

◆ **Small Business Primer**

URL: http://www.ces.ncsu.edu/depts/fcs/business/welcome.html

◆ **Small Business Resource**

http://www.irl.co.uk/sbr

◆ **Smalloffice.com**

http://www.smalloffice.com

Save On Legal Fees

with software and books from Made E-Z Products available at your
nearest bookstore, or call 1-800-822-4566

Stock No.: BK311
$29.95 8.5" x 11"
500 pages Soft cover
ISBN 1-56382-311-X

Everyday Law Made E-Z

The book that saves legal fees every time it's opened.

Here, in *Everyday Law Made E-Z*, are fast answers to 90% of the legal
questions anyone is ever likely to ask, such as:

- How can I control my neighbor's pet?
- Can I change my name?
- What is a common law marriage?
- When should I incorporate my business?
- Is a child responsible for his bills?
- Who owns a husband's gifts to his wife?
- How do I become a naturalized citizen?
- Should I get my divorce in Nevada?
- Can I write my own will?
- Who is responsible when my son drives my car?
- How can my uncle get a Green Card?
- What are the rights of a non-smoker?
- Do I have to let the police search my car?
- What is sexual harassment?
- When is euthanasia legal?
- What repairs must my landlord make?
- What's the difference between fair criticism and slander?
- When can I get my deposit back?
- Can I sue the federal government?
- Am I responsible for a drunken guest's auto accident?
- Is a hotel liable if it does not honor a reservation?
- Does my car fit the lemon law?

Whether for personal or business use, this 500-page information-packed book
helps the layman safeguard his property, avoid disputes, comply with legal
obligations, and enforce his rights. Hundreds of cases illustrate thousands of
points of law, each clearly and completely explained.

ss 1999.r2

Whatever you need to know, we've made it E-Z!

Informative text and forms you can fill out on-screen.* From personal to business, legal to leisure—we've made it E-Z!

PERSONAL & FAMILY

For all your family's needs, we have titles that will help keep you organized and guide you through most every aspect of your personal life.

BUSINESS

Whether you're starting from scratch with a home business or you just want to keep your corporate records in shape, we've got the programs for you.

By the book...

Index

K-P❖❖❖❖

Q-Z❖❖❖❖